Nonviolent Resistance

NONVIOLENT RESISTANCE
A Philosophical Introduction

Todd May

polity

First published in 2015 by Polity Press
Reprint 2016, 2017

Polity Press
65 Bridge Street
Cambridge CB2 1UR, UK

Polity Press
350 Main Street
Malden, MA 02148, USA

ISBN-13: 978-0-7456-7118-5 (hardback)
ISBN-13: 978-0-7456-7119-2 (paperback)

A catalogue record for this book is available from the British Library.

Library of Congress Cataloging-in-Publication Data

May, Todd, 1955–
    Nonviolent resistance : a philosophical introduction / Todd May.
        pages cm
        ISBN 978-0-7456-7118-5 (hardback) – ISBN 0-7456-7118-7 (hardcover)
– ISBN 978-0-7456-7119-2 (paperback)   1. Nonviolence.   2. Nonviolence–
History.   3. Political participation–History.   I. Title.
    HM1281.M395 2015
    303.6′1–dc23
                                    2014025914

Typeset in 10.5 on 12 pt Sabon
by Toppan Best-set Premedia Limited
Printed and bound in the United States by LSC Communications

For further information on Polity, visit our website: politybooks.com

Contents

Preface and Acknowledgments

I began thinking seriously about nonviolence roughly four years before the event that appears on the cover of this book. In January 1985 I joined the River City Nonviolent Resistance Campaign. At my first meeting, there were only two other people there. One of them, Molly Rush, had become famous – infamous to some – as a member of the Plowshares Eight. Along with the Berrigan brothers and several others, in September 1980 Molly entered a weapons facility, damaged nuclear warhead cones, and poured blood on the files there to protest against the Carter Administration's adoption of a "first-strike" policy. That was a policy that allowed the USA to strike first with nuclear weapons, rather than only using them for retaliation. Molly remains the most steadfast proponent of nonviolent resistance I have met. Liane Norman was an organizer, teacher, and writer about nonviolence, who introduced me to a number of texts (including several of hers) that allowed me to study aspects of nonviolence.

That first night we began planning a campaign of protest in the lobby of Westinghouse Electric Company headquarters, which is located in Pittsburgh where I was living. The reason we targeted Westinghouse did not have to do with their production of home appliances. Rather, it concerned their deep involvement in nuclear weapons production. (Later in the campaign, one executive told us that while only about a quarter of Westinghouse's resources were invested in weapons production, nearly half their profit came from it.) The nature of the protest was that it would take place over two weeks.

Each day someone would walk into the lobby of the head-quarters, hold up a sign protesting Westinghouse's nuclear involvement, and wait to be arrested. And, by the way, both Liane and Molly were going to be out of town during the first part of the protests, so could I oversee it? Thus was I plunged into the world of nonviolent resistance. I have since participated in nonviolent campaigns of various sorts to protest against US involvement in Central America, apartheid in South Africa, the Israeli occupation of Palestine, the treatment of labor and labor unions, racism, and the oppression of gays, lesbians, and transsexuals. In recent years my involvement has slackened, mostly due to the difficulty of organizing in the area in which I live. Writing has gradually taken over from organizing, not without some regret. However, until now I have never written anything extended on nonviolence.

The opportunity arose when I was contacted by Polity's Louise Knight. A fellow academic, Brad Evans, had constructed a website (which is still going strong) called historiesofviolence.com. The goal of the website is to reflect on the character of violence in the wake of the 9/11 attacks. Brad asked me to contribute a talk to the website, and I requested to talk on nonviolence rather than violence. The reason for this is that we academics are often very good at critique, but less enthusiastic about framing alternatives. We are past masters at diagnosing what is wrong with a political, economic, or social arrangement, but tend to shy away from asking how it might be addressed. There is perhaps a good reason for this: academics should not be in the business of prescribing for others how to engage in their struggles. However, that precept does not preclude all kinds of reflective activity. My talk was geared toward developing a broad understanding of the role nonviolence has played in many recent struggles against oppression.

After viewing the talk, Louise was kind enough to invite me to submit a proposal for a book on nonviolence to Polity. When she contacted me I realized that although I had spent years in and around nonviolent struggle and even more years studying philosophy, I had never brought the two together. This book is an attempt to rectify that. There is much that has been written about nonviolence, and recent years have seen a minor explosion of literature on the topic from new histories to sociological studies to journal discussions. Some of that literature will be brought to bear in these pages, although I hasten to add that I am not an expert in the vast field of peace studies research. Philosophical reflection on nonviolence, however, has been sparse. (Reflection on violence has been less sparse, as Chapter 2 shows, but neither has it been a central concern of recent philosophy.) What I hope to have contributed here is a first extended philosophical attempt to think about the character of nonviolence, and especially campaigns of nonviolent resistance. My hope is not that this will fill a gap in the philosophical literature, but instead that it will open discussion on an area that is as neglected as it is urgent to think about. With luck, better minds than mine will extend and correct what I have written here in order to develop a rigorous and sustained reflection on what nonviolence is and what prospects it presents for future political engagement.

Between the evening I met Molly and Liane and now, many people have taught me about nonviolent resistance. Their names would fill a chapter of this book. However, I would especially like to thank my long-time friends and fellow activists Mark Lance and Jules Lobel. Moreover, my wife Kathleen has taught me much in this area. Her nonviolent instincts are surer than mine. (I will suggest no more in this direction than that I once earned the nickname Sugar Ray, not for any pugilistic skills – of which I possess none – but for a lapse in nonviolent discipline during a particularly tense political standoff.) More recently, my colleagues Candice Delmas and Chris Grau helped me think more clearly about how to approach the issue of violence, and hence of nonviolence.

I would like to acknowledge Lexington Press for permission to reprint several pages from my article "Kant via Rancière: From Ethics to Anarchism," which appeared in *How Not To Be Governed*, edited by Jimmy Klausen and James Martel.

This book is dedicated to all those whose names have not entered the history books but who have given their time, their bodies, their energy, and sometimes their lives in nonviolent resistance to one or another of the oppressions that have afflicted so many through history, and that continue to plague us today.

1
Vignettes of Nonviolence

In the capital, Tallinn, of the small country of Estonia, there is a large band shell. It can accommodate tens of thousands of people. The band shell can be seen from the top of the castle in Tallinn's Old Town, a complex that was spared the ravages of much of the destruction of World War II. Nestled in the hills outside the center of Tallinn, it is important for Estonians, since singing is part of their culture. Even during the Soviet occupation from 1945 to 1991, Estonians gathered every five years for a festival of song that drew large parts of the country's million-plus population. In fact, the band shell itself was constructed in 1960, during the height of the Soviet occupation. However, on the night of June 11, 1988, the role of song in Estonian life became much more than an expression of Estonian culture. It emerged instead as one of the primary weapons against the Soviet occupation itself.[1]

Earlier that evening, a concert had taken place in the Town Hall Square as part of Tallin's annual "Old Town Days" festival. Since daylight lasts late into the night during the short Estonian summer, those who attended the concert were not ready to call it quits after the music ended. Instead, thousands of them walked the several miles to the grounds of the band shell and began to sing. This in itself would be unremarkable. However, the next night the crowds grew to nearly 100,000 – almost ten per cent of Estonia's population. Moreover, several people – punk rock musicians – displayed the blue, black, and white Estonian national flag, which was banned under the Soviets. And, as one author describes it, "a man on a motorcycle, rock drummer Paap Kõlar, whipped around the perimeter of the amphitheater, moving like an apparition, as the Estonian colors that he carried fluttered above him. The crowd roared. For some young people, this was the first time they had seen their old national flag in public."[2]

For six successive night Estonians gathered at the band shell to sing. Hundreds of thousands of them showed up every night to what was later to be called the "Singing Revolution." Among the most important of their songs was one, based on a nineteenth-century poem and put to music by the composer Gustav Ernesaks, whose English translation is "Land of My Fathers, Land that I Love." It was first performed at the song festival of 1947, its nationalist lyrics somehow escaping the Soviet censors. This is a bit puzzling, since the song laments, "Envy makes strangers slander you / You are still alive in my heart." Over the years, it became the unofficial national anthem of Estonia. Although the Soviets tolerated it, they sought to change the lyrics to be more in accordance with the official "proletarian" orientation of the occupation. However, its lyrics and its significance remained for the Estonian people. Once, in 1969, during the centennial anniversary of the first singing festival in the university town of Tartu, the Soviet authorities decided to ban the song. However, after demanding that it be played, the concert attendees sang it themselves, over and over. Played at every song festival, "Land of My Fathers, Land that I Love" became the centerpiece of Estonian national expression.

The protests in the summer of 1988 did not wane with the dimming of the "White Nights" of summer. On September 10, organized by the resistance group the Popular Front, a singing protest drew 300,000 people, nearly a third of the country's entire population. By this time, the protest movement was in full sway. Speakers at the event railed against the Soviet occupation and asserted the national history of Estonia. At a time when Mikhail Gorbachev was allowing for *glasnost* – openness – the Estonian people were recovering their history and their country through their voices.

In the summer of 1989, one of the most remarkable protests in the history of the Soviet occupation occurred. On

August 23, across the three Baltic republics of Estonia, Latvia, and Lithuania, a human chain of two million hand-holders gathered across 450 miles to protest against their collective occupation. The chain was timed to coincide with the fiftieth anniversary of the Molotov–Ribbentrop Pact, the secret agreement between Hitler and Stalin that divided Eastern Europe into spheres of influence, giving the Baltic States and Finland to the Soviet Union. (The Pact itself was, of course, violated by Hitler when he invaded the Soviet Union.)

In Estonia, resistance to Soviet rule continued. Early in 1990, an alternative Estonian government was created, one that reflected a variety of different parties that had been organizing against the occupation. This alternative government began working on issues of statehood and citizenship in an envisioned independent Estonian polity, in competition with the daily administration emanating from Moscow.

However, as this unfolded, there was resistance not only from the Soviets but from within Estonia itself. Over the course of the occupation, the Soviet Union had adopted a policy of moving ethnic Russians into Estonia, and by the late 1980s they constituted a large percent of the Estonian population, and perhaps half of the population of the capital city of Tallinn. These Russians, far from looking forward to Estonian independence, saw it as a threat. The reason for this – and it is a source of continuing tension in Estonia – is that the Estonian movement did not so much want to *declare* independence as to *restore* it. This means that legal citizenship would only be available to legal descendants of the Estonians who were citizens before the Soviet occupation, effectively excluding the ethnic Russians who were currently living there.

In their turn, then, ethnic Russians began to create their own organizations to counter those developed by ethnic Estonians. In May 1990 the Supreme Council of the alternative Estonian government, in a move that inverted that of the Soviets, declared the hammer-and-sickle flag illegal. This move was publicly criticized by Gorbachev, which in turn prompted the Russian organization, Interfront, to protest in front of the Estonian parliament. The demonstration turned aggressive, with the protestors storming the gates of the building and re-planting the hammer-and-sickle. In response, the head of the parliament, Edgar Savisaar, got on the radio and announced the siege to the wider Estonian population. Thousands of Estonians soon turned up at the site, surrounding the Russians, who were unable to enter the parliament building and were now trapped in the courtyard of the complex.

At this point, it seemed impossible that violence could be avoided. The Interfront protestors had sought to overthrow the Estonian alternative government and replace it with the hated symbols – and reality – of Soviet rule. And they were now caught without any avenue of escape in the courtyard of the building they had sought, in an echo of Soviet rule, to occupy. However, at this moment a remarkable thing happened. Rather than attacking Interfront, the Estonians cleared a path to let them exit peacefully. As they moved through the human corridor that had been cleared for them, although the Estonian crowd shouted at them, none of the Interfront members were touched.

This, of course, was not the end of Soviet rule. The crowning moment came in August, 1991. At that moment in Russia, Soviet hard-liners had temporarily taken control of the government and removed Gorbachev as head of state. On August 20, the Estonian parliament declared independence. This declaration was rejected by the Soviets, who then moved tanks toward Tallinn. In particular, it sought to take over the television tower in order to coordinate its re-occupation and deliver instructions to the population. Realizing this, hundreds of Estonians rushed to surround the tower. Inside were two Estonian police officers. As the Soviet troops threatened to break into the tower, one of the policemen, Jüri Joost, threatened to release Freon from the fire extinguisher system. This would have killed everyone inside the tower, not only the troops but the policemen as well. Remarkably, while the Soviet troops were deciding how to respond to the threat, the coup in Moscow collapsed and the Soviet troops withdrew. Soon after, the new – or, more accurately, renewed – Estonian state was admitted to the United Nations.

The independence movement that finally liberated Estonia from Soviet rule was achieved without violence, even though there were moments that could have tipped the scales toward violent resistance. There were many reasons for this, having to do with the historical character of the Estonian people

– for example, the importance of song in their repertoire of protest – to the specific dynamics of the situation as it unfolded in Estonia and the Soviet Union generally. It was also due to the patient organizing of several organizations that were developed in the 1987–8 period. Among those organizations were the Popular Front and the Estonian National Independence Party (which led one of the first open protests against the Soviet occupation in 1987), but also, and as important, the Estonian Heritage Society. Among the most important tasks for the Estonian people was a recognition of their own history, one that had been silenced throughout the Soviet occupation. This was particularly important for Estonia, since its history is one of occupation by foreign countries. Before the Russians there were the Germans, and before them the Swedes. In fact, until 1991 Estonia was an independent country only between the two World Wars. As significant as political resistance was to its liberation was the task of forming a sense of Estonia as a polity in its own right. The Heritage Society thus became a central player in the Estonian independence movement.

These organizations were often at work behind the scenes in the Singing Revolution and in interaction with the spontaneous events that were unfolding. It would be a mistake to assume too romantically that it was simply the singing that gained Estonian independence. In fact, an Estonian friend of mine, looking back on the events of that period, commented that, "it was just people singing, but suddenly, it was no longer *just* singing, if you see what I mean."[3]

In addition to the organizations and mass protests that were formed during the period leading to independence, there were events of resistance preceding those of the 1987–91 period. We have already seen that, throughout the history of the Soviet occupation, the song "Land of My Fathers, Land that I Love" was a touchstone of resistance, and that the refusal of the Soviet censors to allow it to be sung in 1969 elicited mass resistance among those attending that year's festival. In late 1986 and early 1987, Estonian scientists and students demonstrated against phosphate mining off the shores of Estonia in what became known as the "phosphate war." During the history of the occupation, the Soviets had engaged in exploiting Estonia's resources in environmentally degrading ways. Phosphate mining is a particularly egregious form of such degradation, allowing phosphates to seep into the ground water. It also served to bring in thousands of ethnic Russians as mine workers. The resistance to such mining, before the outbreak of the central events of independence, was successful in forcing the Soviets to cut back on plans to increase the mining of phosphates.

In fact, resistance to the occupation can be traced back to the beginning of the occupation itself. Guerilla fighters, who became known as the Forest Brothers because they would camp in Estonia's many forests, fought against the Soviet invasion of Estonia as they had fought against the Germans in World War II. Eventually, they were decimated, although one of them, August Sabe, survived until 1978 when he was betrayed by a Soviet agent. When he was discovered, he leapt into a river and killed himself.

The more recent history of Estonian resistance, however, those series of events that led to independence, were not the product of violent resistance. Grounded in patient organizing and song, they appealed to the national traditions of Estonia in order to garner the sustained support of the Estonian people – at one moment nearly a third of them – in order to keep alive the history and desires that the Soviets sought to suppress. Further, the use of those traditions was successful not only in re-creating the Estonian nation but also in preventing the kind of violence that would have offered excuses at particular junctures for further Soviet incursion. Finally, and most importantly, by staying within the boundaries of nonviolent activity, the Estonian people crafted a project of national liberation that expressed a dignity that can stand as a benchmark for its further development as a nation.

*

The beginning of the end of the dictatorship of Ferdinand Marcos can be given a specific date: August 21, 1983.[4] On that day, opposition leader Benigno "Ninoy" Aquino stepped off the plane in which he had returned to Manila after three years in exile and was promptly shot dead.

Aquino, the most prominent figure in Filipino resistance to Marcos, espoused nonviolent resistance to the Marcos regime. He had not always done so. After Marcos' declaration of martial law in September 1972, Aquino was arrested and spent the next seven years in detention in a Filipino prison. In 1980 he was sentenced to death, but the discovery of a heart condition led to his release for medical treatment in the United States after intervention on his behalf by the US State Department. While in exile in the USA, Aquino aligned himself with the A6LM movement – the April 6 Liberation Movement. Named after the day in 1978 when Filipinos, to protest against one of Marcos' fraudulent elections, banged pots and pans throughout the night, the A6LM favored bombings and assassinations as means of resistance. These bombings, however, failed to spark a popular revolt, and gradually Aquino began to reconsider his approach. He had become familiar with Gandhi's writings on nonviolence in prison, and a viewing of the film *Gandhi*, which details (a bit romantically) the successful Indian struggle against British occupation, became a turning point for him. In fact, before returning to meet his fate in Manila, Aquino announced that he sought to "join the ranks of those struggling to restore our rights and freedoms through nonviolence."[5] This was, of course, not to be.

Aquino and the A6LM movement were not the only opposition to the Marcos regime. Since the late 1960s, violent resistance movements stemming from both communist and Muslim quarters sought to overthrow his presidency. In fact, it was those movements that provided the excuse for Marcos to declare martial law in September, 1972 and to enjoy the support of the USA and much of the international business community throughout the course of the next fourteen years. However, not all of the opposition to Marcos was rooted in violence. The Catholic Church, particularly under the leadership of Cardinal Jaime Sin, opposed the Marcos regime but denounced violence. Cardinal Sin would play a major role in the events that unfolded after Aquino's assassination. There was also electoral opposition to the dictatorship, but it was weakened by internal divisions and the ongoing fraud that characterized elections under the Marcos regime.

Closer to the date of Aquino's return, the business community began to press Marcos for reforms. His increasing association with corruption led to worries about economic instability. Moreover, the military was developing fissures in response to his penchant for promoting personal friends and allies rather than military professionals to important military posts. This, plus pressure from the USA for a patina of reform, motivated Marcos to declare the lifting of martial law in early 1981 – over nine years after its initial declaration. The lifting of martial law, however, did not result in any changes in power or in the regime's human rights record.

Everything changed, however, in late August of 1983. The murder of an internationally known opposition leader who urged nonviolent change could not be covered up in the eyes of Filipinos or the international community. Two million people turned out for his funeral procession. That single event crystallized the character of the Marcos regime and led to the events that would result, three years later, in his ousting from office.

One of the initial responses actually came from the business community. In September 1983, part of the Filipino business community organized what would become weekly demonstrations against the regime in Manila. Later that month, anti-Marcos demonstrations emerged that at times turned violent. Capital flight began to affect the stability of the regime. However, one of the most important sources of resistance came from an unexpected quarter: Aquino's erstwhile less public wife, Corazón "Cory" Aquino. In the wake of her husband's murder, she became a central figure in the Filipino resistance movement and eventually the first female president of a country in Asia.

Among the most important internal divisions among the various forces opposing the Marcos regime was the disagreement about whether to participate in elections. The elections were, of course, fraudulent. However, if the fraudulence could be exposed, then, some argued, that would further weaken the regime's legitimacy, not only at home but also abroad. In particular, it might raise a challenge to US support, which seemed unwavering during the administration of Ronald Reagan, because of Marcos' uncompromising anti-communism. The 1984 elections for the National Assembly, coming over a year after the assassination of Benito Aquino, provided a test case for the effectiveness of this strategy. While the communist-oriented groups decided to boycott the election, several of the more liberal groups, including Cory Aquino's, opted to participate. The results of the election gave 30 percent of the seats to the opposition, with Marcos' party retaining 70 percent, down from the previous 90 percent. The key player in this election, however, was not the opposition but a group called the National Movement of Citizens for a Free Election, or NAMFREL. NAMFREL was an election-monitoring group that was originally formed by the Central Intelligence Agency in the early 1950s and was revived in 1983 by a coalition of businesspeople, professionals, religious groups, and others. Their goal was to provide an independent monitoring of elections in competition with the government-approved agency. In the 1984 elections, they turned out 200,000 volunteers. Moreover, in those districts where they were able to monitor the vote, the opposition was declared to have won over 60 percent of the vote. NAMFREL, then, provided two services to the opposition. First, it kept an independent eye on the electoral process. Second, it gave hope to the opposition that there was enough grassroots support to sustain the strategy of electoral participation.

Such participation was not the only element of opposition strategy. In addition to rallies and continued violent resistance, there were a series of strikes – *welgang bayan*, or "people's strikes" – organized by the leftist groups that were not participating in the electoral process. These strikes were enormously effective, often involving large sectors of the economic community. "By the end of 1984, transportation strikes paralyzed areas of metropolitan Manila and Central Luzon, as well as southern cities, such as Davao, Butuan, Cagayan de Oro, Bacolod, and Cebu. In December 1984 a *welgang bayan* in Bataan shut down approximately 80 percent of transportation in the entire province."[6] For Marcos, the combination of opposition tactics, in addition to capital flight, was threatening to undermine his ability to hold on to power.

The next presidential elections were scheduled for 1987 but, seeing the erosion of his authority, Marcos decided to call for early elections, in February 1986. Early elections would not only prop up his failing status, they would also prevent the opposition from having time to organize. It was a tactical mistake on his part. Much of the opposition rallied around Corazón Aquino as the opposition candidate, and their campaign was well organized and run. The campaign culminated in a rally three days before the election that drew over a million people. By election day, it was evident that Marcos could not win without massive fraud, which he then engaged in. NAMFREL declared Aquino's UNIDO (United Democratic Action Organization) the winner in the 70 percent of provinces where they were allowed to operate, but Marcos' own group gave him the victory. However, there was dissent even within his own organization: after seeing elections discrepancies, over thirty technicians from the government-controlled monitoring group walked out on the process.

The day after the election, a million and a half people rallied in Manila's Luneta Park to protest against the election results. Aquino addressed the rally. "If Goliath refuses to yield," she announced, "we shall escalate. I am not calling for violent revolution. This is not the time for that. I always indicated that now is the way of nonviolent struggle for justice. This means active resistance to evil by peaceful means."[7]

This nonviolent struggle, involving boycotts, rallies, defections from Marcos' government, bank withdrawals, and other means, culminated a mere two weeks after the election. The final crisis began on February 22. It was centered on the Filipino military. Juan Ponce Enrile, a former member of Marcos' military inner circle, had been planning a coup to overthrow the dictator in 1985. However, in the wake of Marcos' surprise announcement of elections, they scrapped their plans, hoping that the election itself might end his rule. (Enrile's motives were not entirely altruistic. He was bitter at being passed over for heading the military when Marcos declared martial law in 1972, and had been plotting since then.) Enrile knew that in the chaos after the election he might be a target for assassination, and several of his compatriots confirmed this on the 22nd. So he took his 400 troops and occupied the defense ministry headquarters in Manila. From there he called the current head of the Filipino military, Fidel Ramos, to inform him of what he had done and to ask for his support. Ramos offered his support and joined Enrile at the defense headquarters. Together they held a press conference declaring the Marcos regime to be illegitimate and announcing their support of Corazón Aquino.

The reaction from Marcos and the military loyal to him, they knew, would not be long in coming. So they called Cardinal Sin, who had long counseled nonviolent resistance against the regime, for support. Cardinal Sin, in turn, announced the defection on the radio and called for civilian support for the rebel soldiers. Immediately, thousands showed up to erect barricades and block the anticipated invasion with their bodies. Sure enough, after trading radio and television ultimatums with Enrile and Ramos, Marcos sent in his military to take back the defense ministry. They were met by 50,000 chanting protestors who refused to disperse and refused to engage in any violence against the soldiers. In fact, the protestors, in an echo of earlier anti-war protests in the United States, offered the invading soldiers chocolate and flowers.

The invaders hesitated, and then relented. No shots were fired. Generals ordered to attack the protestors and the defense headquarters defected. Two days later, officials from the Reagan administration, which had been steadfast in its support of Marcos, told him that the time had come for him to step down. On February 25, Corazón Aquino was sworn in as President and Ferdinand Marcos escorted by his erstwhile US supporters to live in exile in Hawaii.

The nonviolent discipline displayed by those who occupied the area around the defense headquarters was steadfast. It did not, of course, arise entirely spontaneously. Among the protestors were many religious followers of Cardinal Sin, businesspeople who had opposed Marcos for years, and other Filipinos who had lived through the violence of both the Marcos years and the communist rebellion. And their leaders – not only Sin, but also Aquino, who followed her late husband in this – were committed to nonviolence. In this case, not only did the nonviolence prevent military intervention, it also protected a military group that would have been unable to defend itself had it been attacked. The irony was recognized by Enrile himself, who said, "It was funny. We in the defense and military organization who should be protecting the people were being protected by them."[8]

*

January 25 was declared National Police Day by the former Egyptian dictator Hosni Mubarak in 2009. The memorial was to commemorate the British army massacre of Egyptian police on that day in 1952 when fifty officers were killed after refusing to surrender the weapons in their police station. Mubarak's purpose in announcing the holiday was to offer public recognition to Egypt's security services, services which helped sustain his presidency and therefore had earned more gratitude from him than from the Egyptian populace at large. In one of those ironic twists of history, two years later the same date would spell the beginning of the end of the Mubarak regime.[9]

The demonstration on January 25, 2011 was not a secret. It had been announced on various social media, and there were security services there to stop it. One participant from the April 6 Youth Movement (to which we will return in a moment) had posted a video announcing, "I, a girl, am going down to Tahrir Square and I will stand alone ... and I'll hold up a banner, perhaps [other] people will show some honor."[10] However, the demonstrators had developed tactics to evade the police. Organizers from the demonstration were trained in nonviolence. At least one of them, Mohammed Adel, had received tactical nonviolence training in Serbia, where a non-violent revolution grounded in the views of Gene Sharp (whom we will meet later in this book) had played a central role in the overthrow of the dictator Slobodan Milosevic. Rather than seeking to gather together in a central location, dispersed groups were sent to Tahrir Square in central Cairo at various times. Many of them did not get through, but many others did, particularly those from a working-class neighborhood that had evaded the dispersed police presence. This group, which by the time it reached the Square numbered in the thousands, took up the chant of the Tunisian revolution of the month before: "The people want to bring down the regime."

These were heady days in what was to come to be known as the Arab Spring. It had started a month before in the town of Sidi Bouzid in Tunisia. On December 17, 2010, Muhammed Bouazizi, a street vendor, set himself on fire in front of a local government building. The events precipitating his self-immolation are not entirely clear. In response to some unknown provocation, a policewoman had taken his belongings, and perhaps had slapped him in the process. And for whatever reason, this was the last straw for Muhammed Bouazizi. He ended his life in public protest and, as he certainly could not have foreseen, began a wave of protests that stretched from Tunisia to Egypt and after that across the Arab world as far as Libya and Syria that was to change the character of the region. Why it was this particular act of protest – or of desperation – that set the events of the Arab Spring in motion will likely remain a subject of debate. Why did Rosa Parks' decision in Montgomery, Alabama in December of 1955, set in motion the Montgomery Bus Boycott and the subsequent American Civil Rights Movement? There had been others before her who had been arrested for refusal to yield their seats to a white person. And in Tunisia there had been others who protested at the dictatorial regime of Zine al-Abidine Ben Ali or the conditions over which he presided, if perhaps not in so striking a way. Some acts shift the ground like underwater tectonic plates creating a tsunami, while others cause barely a tremble.

Of course, Bouazizi's act would not have had the effect it did had the Tunisians not been ready for political change. The Tunisian Revolution, in turn, would not have had the effect it did in Egypt had the Egyptians themselves not been prepared. That preparation involved more than disgust with the Mubarak regime, corrupt as it was. And it involved more than the increasing misery caused by the neoliberal policies championed by the United States and other supporters of the regime, although that played a large role in stirring Egyptian dissatisfaction. As historians Lin Nouehid and Alex Warren note, "The privatization policies that were so lauded by the IMF were perceived by Egyptians as no more than a ploy by Mubarak and his cronies to line their pockets at the expense of the people and their national economy."[11] For there to be a regime change, there had to be more. In a country as large and populous as Egypt, where the events of Tahrir Square would be replicated in dozens and perhaps hundreds of towns and villages, sustained resistance required organization and expertise. The Egyptians had both in good measure. While the events in Tahrir Square following the January 25 demonstration unfolded in a spontaneous way, they emerged from a ground that was well seeded.

Demonstrations in the Arab world in support of Palestinian rights and against US policy in the region had been commonplace. In 2000, with the onset of the second Palestinian *intifada*, there were a number of demonstrations of support in Egypt. These demonstrations, which also appeared three years later when the USA invaded Iraq, called themselves the *Kefaya* ("Enough") movement. However, what was stirring in this movement was that it was not only "enough" with regard to the Israeli occupation or US intervention into the region, but also with regard to the ongoing state of emergency under which Mubarak ruled Egypt, imprisoned opposition figures, and enriched himself and those around him.

These stirrings broke out in December 2006, when a strike at Egypt's largest textile factory undertaken by between 24,000 and 28,000 workers won them bonuses that had been promised earlier but never paid. There were thousands of strikes over the next five years. These strikes not only challenged the economic conditions of workers; they also laid the organizational groundwork for the events of 2011. For instance, one of the most active groups in Tahrir Square – the April 6 Youth Movement – grew out of the efforts of Egyptian youth to support another strike in the industrial town of Al-Mahalla Al-Kobra, the same town that saw the December, 2006 textile strike. The April 6 movement began to organize online, developing a network of supporters and organizers that would be unleashed during the early months of 2011. It is significant that the group's symbol, a raised fist, was exactly the same symbol used by the Serbian nonviolent resistance movement against Slobodan Milosevic. In fact, Mohammed Adel, the activist who studied nonviolence in Serbia, was one of the central organizers in the April 6 movement.

The efforts of April 6 – and of the Egyptian resistance movement generally – were fueled by the police murder of a young activist in Alexandria, Khaled Said. In June 2010, police entered a café in which Said was relaxing, and, in front of numerous witnesses, dragged him out of the café and beat him to death. A picture of his grossly disfigured head, taken in the morgue, went viral on a webpage entitled "We are all

Khaled Said." The webpage itself was maintained by Wael Ghonim, who, along with members of the April 6 Youth Movement, members of the Muslim brotherhood, and labor organizers, originally called for the demonstration in Tahrir Square on January 25.

The occupation of Tahrir Square did not begin entirely nonviolently. There were fights between some protestors and police, and reports of a few Molotov cocktails being thrown. Although many of the organizers were coming from a position of nonviolence, the size of the demonstrations and the varied backgrounds of the demonstrators meant that they could not be trained and organized toward the same orientation. However, in the initial days of the protest, there was also internal discord in Mubarak's internal security apparatus. After the success of the January 25 protest, another one was announced for three days later. The success of the second protest in occupying Tahrir Square exasperated Mubarak himself, who called for the police to fire live ammunition at protestors. When the interior minister's deputy refused to heed the call, Mubarak instead called for the army to enter the square, at which point the interior minister, in pique at being marginalized, withdrew the police before the army arrived, allowing time for protestors to cement their occupation of the square.

The Egyptian army plays an outsized role in the politics of Egypt. Although it is technically under the command of the president, it considers itself a more independent force. Also, since many Egyptians have served in the military, there is a closer relationship between the military and the populace than between the police force and the populace. When the military entered Tahrir Square on January 28, it was greeted not with fists and Molotov cocktails but with flowers and cheering. The crowds occupying the square felt that the military would not use force against them in the way the internal security apparatus of the police had. In this, they were right. The army announced that it would not fire on protestors, thus effectively granting them the ability to remain in Tahrir Square.

However, Mubarak had no intention of relinquishing office, and no intention of allowing the protestors to remain in Tahrir Square. Bereft of army support to disperse the protestors, he and his supporters turned to paid looters and criminals in order to infiltrate and disrupt the demonstration and encampment. February 2 saw "the Battle of the Camels" when camel riders who usually give rides to tourists to view the pyramids were hired to attack the protestors. Throughout the provocations, however, the protestors remained largely nonviolent, refusing the authorities an excuse to intervene and continuing to justify the army's forbearance.

As the days passed, the conflict between Mubarak and the protestors became one of attrition. He would not leave office and they would not leave Tahrir Square. The question was one of who could outlast whom. A continuing standoff favored Mubarak, since sooner or later the demonstrators would be seen as having failed. And this became evident as the days passed without movement on either side. Then, on February 7, Wael Ghonim, the founder of the website "We are all Khaled Said" was released after a week and a half in jail. He appeared on television and gave an impassioned critique of the government and support to the protests. This reinvigorated the movement and brought thousands more demonstrators to the square. In addition – and partly in response to Ghonim's speech – independent labor organizations started supporting the movement through the initiation of strikes. Until then, because the main labor union was under government control, many workers had been on the sidelines of the protests in Tahrir Square and around Egypt. However, within a few days of Ghonim's speech there was an effective general strike in Egypt, and on February 11, eighteen days into the occupation of Tahrir Square, Mubarak's vice president Omar Suleiman announced on television, "Taking into consideration the difficult circumstances the country is going through, President Mohammed Hosni Mubarak has decided to leave the post of president and has tasked the Supreme Council of the Armed Forces to manage the state's affairs."[12]

What happened in Tahrir Square? Was it, as the theorist Hamid Dabashi has claimed, the end of decades of reaction against colonialism known as the "postcolonial"? "These revolutionary uprisings," he writes of the Arab Spring, "are postideological, meaning that they are no longer fighting in terms dictated by their condition of coloniality, codenamed

'postcolonial.' "[13] Or instead does it conform to the less san-
guine conclusion offered by Noueihed and Warren that, "By
the end of 2011, what happened in Egypt had amounted not
to a fully-fledged revolution but to a protest-inspired coup
that had removed certain figureheads but left the reins of
power in the hands of a military junta that appeared resistant
to reform and keen to limit change"?[14] The events subsequent
to Tahrir Square would seem to tilt toward a more pessimistic
picture. The army removed an elected, if unpopular, president
and at the moment of this writing rules the country more
directly. However, there have been protests against their rule,
and the events of Tahrir Square have increased organizers'
experience and likely their expertise. Tahrir Square has
entered into the collective memory of Egyptians, and, in the
surprising and unexpected way in which these things happen,
may break out again, in Tahrir Square itself or elsewhere.
After all, who would have expected that a street vendor's
setting himself alight in a small town in Tunisia would result
in the removal of heads of state from Tunisia to Libya?

*

They didn't look like a group that would change the discussion of wealth in America when they gathered at Zuccotti
Park near Wall Street in lower Manhattan on September 17,
2011. In fact, as their number grew, they reflected a segment
of the population that was overwhelmingly white and middle
class.[15] Often a bit ragged around the edges, partly from
personal taste and eventually from sleeping in the park for
weeks on end, the participants in the New York Occupy
movement were not the picture one generally has of opinion-
makers. And yet they, and their aligned occupations around
the country, brought the issue of the disparities of US wealth
to public discussion with an urgency that it had not seen
before in this period of growing wealth inequality.

The original protest itself emerged from several sources,
the most prominent of which is probably the Canadian anti-
consumerist group Adbusters.[16] Inspired by the anti-austerity
protests in Greece and especially the occupation of Tahrir
Square during the Arab Spring, Occupy was initially an
attempt to confront issues of corporate, and especially,

financial warping of the political system of the USA. It quickly adopted the slogan, ascribed to anarchist writer and organizer David Graeber, "We are the 99%." This slogan proved to be one of the most enduring aspects of Occupy, and has been repeated as a mantra numerous times since its coining. It reflects the wealth disparity that characterizes the USA, and did so in a way that allowed many people to see their alliance with protestors with whom they might not otherwise have had any sense of identification.

There are two aspects to Occupy that should be highlighted. First, it did not have at any point in its existence a programmatic set of demands. Twelve days into the protest, it did issue a "Declaration of the Occupation of New York City," a document that seeks to call attention to the ways in which "corporations, which place profit over people, self-interest over justice, and oppression over equality, run our governments." And it lists many of the ways in which corporations do so.[17] But it never makes any specific demands. Rather, it calls upon people to "Exercise your right to peaceably assemble; occupy public space; create a process to address the problems we face, and generate solutions accessible to everyone."

This lack of a set of concrete demands was seen as a failure of vision by many on the left.[18] After all, it was argued, how could people coalesce around a movement that wasn't exactly asking for anything, and how could those in power respond to demands if there were no demands to which to respond? However, as it turns out, it was precisely the lack of demands that was part of the genius of Occupy. Because it had a slogan to which almost everyone could relate and because it did not ask for anything specific, it allowed Americans in various walks of life to identify with it. It was, in a sense, like a green screen upon which people could project their specific marginalizations, oppressions, and exploitations, while at the same time seeing themselves as members of a larger social group, one that has common ground in being taken advantage of by those in power. Although there are limitations in the long term to such a strategy, over the course of the occupation itself (which lasted until November 15, when it was cleared by the police with 200 arrests) it provided a form of solidarity that had been lacking on the left for many years. To see its effectiveness, one can contrast the influence that Occupy had with that of a protest earlier that year in New York, on May 12, when thousands of marchers organized by unions and civic organizations descended on Wall Street to protest against wealth disparities and offered a concrete plan to ameliorate them. That march was soon forgotten; however, Occupy is still discussed.[19]

The strategy of not making specific demands, in addition to allowing vast swathes of the American public to see itself in the movement, also had the effect of encouraging people to organize and make their own demands. In this sense, Occupy has been radically democratic. It does not tell people what they should be asking for, but rather asks them to think through their own local conditions and situation in order to come up with their own strategies and solutions. Although there is a common adversary – corporate and especially financial influence on our political and social fabric – the task is not to follow the leaders of Occupy but instead to develop emancipatory strategies of one's own, in the context in which one lives.

This radically democratic character of Occupy was also reflected in its own internal workings, which is the second aspect of Occupy that should be highlighted. In fact, here is where the nonviolence of Occupy comes to the fore. As one occupant put it, " 'Many participants are consciously prefiguring the kind of society they want to live in.' "[20] Prefiguration is a concept often associated with anarchism. The idea is that the form of resistance one engages in must reflect the kind of society one seeks to live in. This is in contrast to many of the Marxist oriented struggles of the twentieth century. For the latter, the struggle for revolution was entirely separate from the process of living together after the revolution. Struggle was to be conducted in a hierarchical manner with a disciplined group of revolutionaries ordered hierarchically in a military manner. After the state was conquered, then people would re-order their lives into a nonhierarchical social order. As many anarchists stretching back to the nineteenth century revolutionary Mikhail Bakunin argued, the assumption that a revolutionary group, once in power, would voluntarily relinquish it is naive. The revolutions of the twentieth century proved this criticism to be accurate.

What anarchists argue, and what Occupy instantiated, is that the society one wants to see after struggle must be created in the struggle itself. Or, to put it another way, the society one envisions must be *prefigured* in the struggle. If one wants an inclusive society in which everyone can participate in decision-making, this cannot be put off until after resistance has ended; the resistance itself must be organized in order to allow for it. As professor of journalism (and founding member of Students for a Democratic Society) Todd Gitlin put the point, "[t]he talk about 'prefigurations' and 'models' and 'intimations' was not idle, either. It expressed a passion, a will to believe, that it was possible on one patch of ground, even provisionally, even approximately, to plant a foot in a future of active engagement and free expression even (or especially) for those not used to commanding attention – *empowerment*, in a word."[21]

In accordance with the concept of prefiguration, all major decisions were made by a form of consensus in a General Assembly. This involved the often remarked-upon series of hand signals ("twinkles" for agreement, triangles for points of process, etc.). The General Assembly was also the source of the famous "mic check." Since bullhorns and microphones were prohibited by the police, the Occupiers developed an oral process in which the words of the speaker were repeated by those near him and then by those progressively further away in order for everyone to be able to hear them. This not only had the effect of communicating the speaker's words; as one participant in Occupy told me, by repeating the words of the speaker one also had, for a moment, to take on the perspective of the speaker. So that even if one disagreed with the speakers, by repeating their words, their ideas were taken seriously. This allowed for more respectful exchange among participants in conversations about policy.

One of the reasons the New York Occupy worked as well as it did was the relationship that was developed between the process of decision-making and the personal commitment toward others. The former cannot work without the latter; that is, a consensual decision-making process requires that people respect one another's view and display a sense of judgment in deciding whether to go along with a majority view or to block it by refusing consensus.[22] In New York, I was told by one of the participants, there were many people, among them many anarchists, who spent time with other participants educating them about the process of decision-making in order to ensure as smooth a process of meeting as possible. This does not mean there weren't frustrations. One of the organizers notes how "the original General Assembly, which had been intentionally built, could not withstand the pressures of a constant public and permeable space,"[23] and so alternative structures were tested in order to relieve the pressure on the General Assembly. However, New York Occupy was able to sustain a larger participatory structure for a good part of their occupation in part because of the relationship between individual respect and group decision-making. This is in contrast to some of the other occupations, for instance in Los Angeles, where a former student of mine who was a central organizer there expressed his frustration to me over participants who would block the group consensus on every issue, so that the group could not move forward.

This respect shown toward one another through the General Assemblies was not only effective in making its internal workings nonviolent; it also expressed a general nonviolent orientation that was characteristic of its dealings with those outside Occupy. As Gitlin remarks, "Occupy's nonviolence was style, a self-presentation, but it was more than a performance ... It ran deeper, expressing some inner conviction, a sense of dignity that people reached in this movement, some sense that they were, whether taken one at a time or *en masse*, inviolable, that they would only lower themselves if they replied in kind to the violence they received."[24] (We will return to extensive discussion the different meanings of the word *dignity* later.) Here we can see prefiguration in play in another way. Not only were relations with others to reflect the kind of society Occupy sought to achieve, but in addition individuals placed upon themselves the expectation that they should personally act in accordance with that vision. One should *be* the person one seeks to achieve. Or, as the cliché goes, be the change you want to see.

This nonviolence was in evidence throughout much of the New York encampment, and even appeared in the response to the police clearing of Zuccotti Park on November 15, two months after the occupation started.[25] Although there was resistance to the clearing, there was no rioting, nor were there the kinds of violent confrontations that appeared in Oakland, where the relations between occupiers and the police were far more strained. However, this did not stop the police from arresting around a couple of hundred people, including journalists.

*

We commonly think of the twentieth century as an extraordinarily violent one. After the optimism about human progress that characterized much of nineteenth-century thought, the following hundred years gave a more sober cast to considerations about the perfectibility of the human character and human society. In retrospect, the twentieth century seems to have been bathed in blood from one end to the other. Two World Wars, the Holocaust, Stalinism, Maoism, Nazism, proxy wars fought by the USA and USSR in Third World Countries, and the continuing imminent threat of nuclear annihilation: these seems to be the dominant political moments of the century just past.

However, there is another century hidden beneath that one, a century that may not be as widely known but that offers far more promise for the future. That is the history of nonviolence. As Peter Ackerman and Jack DuVall show in their magisterial history of nonviolence in the twentieth century, *A Force More Powerful,* nonviolent resistance and struggle marched step by step alongside the violence that seems to have overshadowed it. If the period from 1900–2000 brought us mass slaughter, it also brought us Gandhi and the Indian Independence Movement, and from there the first systematic thought and practice of nonviolence. From Gandhi in India to the American Civil Rights Movement to Solidarity in Poland to the first Intifada in Palestine to the resistance to dictators like Ferdinand Marcos and the Burmese military to Tiananmen Square to the "color" revolutions in Eastern Europe to Tahrir Square to Occupy, nonviolence evolved from a tactic that emerged here and there in struggle to a body of work that could be studied, emulated, and developed in a coordinated fashion.

This body of work was first articulated in a coordinated way in 1973 by Gene Sharp in his three-volume *The Politics of Nonviolent Action*, a work to which we will return in the third chapter of this book. Sharp's views have been enormously influential, having been used in the Serbian overthrow of Slobodan Milosevic, and from there having been picked up by organizers of Tahrir Square, just as Martin Luther King studied and preached the nonviolent approach of Mohandas Gandhi. This rhizomatic movement of theory, tactics, and strategy is now characteristic of nonviolent practice. When people engage in nonviolence, they study and refer to previous movements and the orientations and operations of those movements. But none of this would have happened had it not been for the trajectory of nonviolent action over the course of the twentieth century. Thanks to the people and movements of that century, we are now the recipients of a *tradition* of nonviolence rather than merely a collection of nonviolent moments.

This tradition, like many traditions, has its privileged elements. Among those elements, two stand out as touchstones: the Indian Independence Movement and the American Civil Rights Movement. And within these, there are particular moments that stand as exemplars of nonviolence. In the Indian Independence Movement, the Salt March of 1930 continues to provide inspiration to those who resist. The Salt March began when Gandhi argued that, in violation of British legal monopoly on salt, Indians should produce their own salt, and he announced that he would lead a march to the sea where Indians could do so. The march lasted twenty-four days, wound through numerous villages, and covered hundreds of miles. It started with seventy people associated with Gandhi's ashram and peaked at 50,000 when he reached the seaside village of Dandi.[26] The Salt March, perhaps more than any other event, was the spark that lit the struggle for independence. It involved not only organizers from the elite strata of Indian society but also villagers who had not been included in the struggle before, and it symbolized in a concrete way the independence from British rule that was the goal of the movement.

The American Civil Rights Movement presents its own set of iconic images.[27] There were Freedom Riders, who violated segregation laws by traveling through the South in racially integrated groups and were met with violent beatings in places like Anniston, Alabama. There were the protestors in Birmingham, who suffered the water cannons and police dogs ordered by Police Chief Bull Connor. There were the lonely walks through vicious chanting crowds by those who sought integrated education, for instance James Meredith at the University of Mississippi. For me, the outstanding image is that of the lunch counter protestors. These were racially integrated groups who would sit at segregated lunch counters and seek to order lunch. They were, of course, refused service, and were smeared with food and beaten by those who sought to maintain racial segregation. However, their quiet dignity and refusal to retaliate in the face of attempted humiliation has always moved and inspired me.

What is it that makes these movements and the images associated with them so compelling? Why do they strike many of us as exemplifying some of the more noble aspects of human capacity? We should not take the answer to these questions as obvious. After all, there is something in the vulnerability of nonviolent protests that actually cuts against the grain of much of Western orientation, particularly in its more masculine variants. In my own country of the United States, there is a great value placed upon winning, and winning is often thought of as vanquishing one's opponent. Currently, the most popular sport in the USA is football. It has replaced baseball as the national pastime. As I write these lines, there is a controversy concerning the widespread prevalence of concussions among former professional players and their long-term impact. Several players have committed suicide and others suffer from severe headaches and memory loss. It seems that it is nearly impossible to play the sport without putting one's future mental health at great risk.

This has led some journalists to call for banning the sport. However, that is a minority view. Even those who would favor a ban recognize its central role in American life. That role is not divorced from the sport's violence. Toughness is a value associated with football, as it is with the military. A player is expected to "suck it up," not complain about injury and return to the field of football battle. Even some players who have suffered long-term mental loss have said that they would not have traded their football career for another one. There is something gladiatorial about American football, and the protections for players that have recently been enacted – meager as they are relative to the injuries players regularly sustain – are sometimes greeted with ambivalence, as though limiting the violence of the game was a stain upon its purity.

We often value military participation for much the same reason. Several of my friends from other countries have expressed puzzlement at America's overbearing focus upon military participation and pride in military conflict. We celebrate a number of major military holidays; soldiers in uniform are offered to board airline flights before other customers; and any critique of the military is seen as a slur upon the country itself. We in the USA give pride of place to a military that, after all, outspends the rest of the industrial world.[28] The military, like football, seems inseparable from a culture for which prevailing under conditions of violence is a test of manhood rather than an indication of a situation that is in need of rectification.

However, a closer look reveals that there is a bond between what is valued in these types of violence and the participation in nonviolent activity that can be one source of its appeal. The toughness that is valued in American football and military participation is not simply a matter of how much pain one can inflict. Rather, and more importantly, it concerns how much pain one can undergo. Toughness is displayed in the ability to sustain injury or violence without being broken by it. It is displayed in the ability to keep one's wits about one and one's focus on the goal under conditions of severe strain. In this sense, toughness is very much like the particular vulnerability displayed in nonviolent struggle and resistance. After all, that vulnerability is not vulnerability in the sense of fragility. It is, rather, quite the opposite.

When the Estonians began to gather for protest marches and then singing their adopted national song, or when the Filipino people blocked the tanks that were headed toward the defense ministry, what they offered to their adversaries was precisely a form of toughness. It was the toughness of those who could bear violence against them. Their "toughness" was greater than that of a football player's or even a soldier's. They were able to face violence without weapons and without protection. They asserted themselves in the full recognition that, were they to be attacked, they would be unable to defend themselves. (To a lesser extent, those who exposed themselves to the elements in the two months of New York Occupy displayed a willingness to undergo physical exposure without complaint.) There is a fortitude to such behavior that is surely the equal to those who seek to counter their vulnerability with armor or weapons.

However, to see nonviolent resistance solely in terms of toughness is to capture only part of what makes it compelling. Nonviolence is more than just some masculine value of toughness displayed in another arena. After all, the toughness displayed in American football or the military is in the service of vanquishing others, and doing so by violence. We might say that their toughness allows them to commit violence, not in the moral sense of giving them permission but in the physical sense of making it possible. Things are different with nonviolence. The toughness of nonviolence consists in *refraining* from committing violence toward others. It consists in undergoing, or at least being willing to undergo, what one does not allow oneself to perform. In this sense, nonviolence has an asymmetrical relation to violence. Unlike football or the military, there is no permission for violence on both sides. To be nonviolent is to refuse oneself access to the violence to which one's adversary feels entitled. This does not entail – as we will see briefly in the following chapter and more fully in the third one – that nonviolence is never coercive. Often it is, particularly when it is successful. However, whatever means of coercion it uses, it cannot resort to violence, which means it does not permit itself means to reach its ends to which its adversaries often help themselves.

This asymmetry reveals something deeper about nonviolence, something that contrasts it more starkly with violent activities. Nonviolence involves a model of how others should be treated. Although we will develop this model more completely in the second, fourth, and fifth chapters, we can indicate something of it here. If nonviolence refuses to act violently against others, there must be a reason for this. It is not simply a game in which one handicaps oneself for the sheer challenge of it. This reason consists in a vision of how it is that people ought to be treated. To refuse violence toward another is to recognize that there is something about the other to be respected. It is to see the other not simply as an obstacle to one's ends, but, as the philosopher Immanuel Kant would have it, as an end in himself or herself. To be sure, violent activities have their moral limits. In football and even in war one cannot do just anything to one's adversary. And to that extent it might be said that even many violent activities recognize a certain inviolability of the other. However, that inviolability is much more minimal, and it operates differently from the way it works in nonviolence. In violent activities, the inviolability of the other is only a limit, a threshold of cruelty that one must not cross. It does not structure the activity but instead merely sets parameters for it.

By contrast, with nonviolence the inviolability of the other, in addition to having a much higher threshold, is also more intimately woven into the activities that constitute its struggle. It does not simply limit one's activity but also structures it. In the case of the Philippines and in Tahrir Square, it dictated the way participants acted toward the police and the military. One does not simply refrain from striking out at them – a futile activity, and one that might offer an excuse for greater violence from their side – but also one seeks to convert them, to make them see as equals to oneself that they are mistaken. Even such symbols as offering chocolate and flowers, as the Filipinos did in front of the defense ministry, indicate a positive relation to their adversaries that was much more than simply a limit on what they could do *to* them.

This is not to argue for a purity of nonviolence either in motive or in deed. Nonviolence, as we will see, can be pragmatic rather than principled. It can be engaged in for reasons that have to do more with calculations about what would likely succeed than with any feeling of respect for one's adversary. And it is rarely, if ever, conducted without elements of violence. Nonviolent discipline, after all, is extraordinarily difficult to maintain, particularly in the face of relentless violence from the other side. However, neither of these shortcomings undermine the particular character of nonviolence. The latter indicates only its difficulty. To sustain a nonviolent vision and nonviolent activity, particularly in a world awash in violence – a world where violence is routinely justified – is psychologically and physically demanding. It requires a form of self-control that can often only be had through rigorous practice. It is difficult then to expect that, particularly in a mass movement, all of the participants will be able to maintain nonviolent discipline, or in some cases will even be interested in maintaining it. The Estonian protests and the Filipino defense of the renegade soldiers were more nearly exceptional in that regard, and, unlike Tahrir Square or even the American Civil Rights Movement or the Indian Independence Movement.

Just as nonviolent movements are rarely purely nonviolent, they are rarely animated by a purely respectful attitude toward the adversary. In the next chapter we will see the difference between principled and practical nonviolence, between nonviolence that is conducted out of a sense of being morally required to be nonviolent and nonviolence adopted for purely strategic reasons, i.e. that it is more likely to be successful. In situations where the adversary holds overwhelming military power, the adoption of nonviolence might seem as much of a necessity as anything else. Since meeting physical force with physical force is unlikely to succeed, nonviolence might appear to be a more attractive option to many, even those who have no respect for the adversary. Or it might be that the adversary is particularly vulnerable to nonviolent action for one reason or another, say it already has a diminished standing in the eyes of outsiders upon whom it is dependent for support. In cases like these the motives driving nonviolent struggle might hardly be distinguishable from those that underlie violent struggle: nonviolent struggle is chosen simply as the best available means of achieving a particular goal.

However, as we will see, even impurely motivated nonviolence exhibits a type of respect for the other, in behavior if not in spirit. And often that respect, empty as it might seem, can have its own consequences for the actors; acting nonviolently can promote a nonviolent attitude. Not only can nonviolent behavior emerge from an attitude of respect for the other. Things can also happen the other way around: nonviolent behavior can generate a nonviolent attitude in its participants.

If nonviolence struggle treats the other with respect, it also and just as insistently expresses the self-respect of participants, an expression we will see in more detail in the fourth and fifth chapters. To stand up against another without weapons, respecting the dignity of the other, is at the same moment a gesture of self-respect. The vulnerability of nonviolence, then, although, as we have seen, asymmetrical in its use of force, is symmetrical in its treatment of participant and adversary in this sense: it not only sees the other as equal to oneself (and therefore worthy of respect), but also sees oneself as equal to the other. One does not stand up to another in one's vulnerability, facing the other person to person – as is often literally the case, for example in the Filipino protests or those in Tahrir Square – without a sense of oneself as equal to those one opposes. Nowhere is this better exemplified than in many of the actions of the American Civil Rights Movement. To sit at a lunch counter or ride a bus or seek to register to vote alongside whites was, for black Americans, an assertion of equality. Moreover, undergoing violence without retribution, as long as one keeps one's "eyes on the prize" (as the phrase went in the Civil Rights Movement), is not a sign of weakness, but rather one of strength. It expresses the esteem in which one holds oneself and one's goals without seeking to diminish the adversary in their humanity.

Of course, by resorting to violence, the adversary might well diminish himself, herself, or themselves. But by remaining nonviolent, actors keep the offer of a return to the moral fold open. Those who have demeaned themselves by violent reaction against nonviolent protestors, because their violence is not returned, retain the possibility of abjuring further violence – even perhaps atoning for it – and raising themselves to the level of moral rectitude that is being offered to them by the protestors themselves.

Nonviolence, then, is a form of struggle that expresses respect for the dignity of all and a presupposition of the equality of everyone. The task of this book is to reflect on this and to offer a general philosophical account of nonviolence. Of course, the first challenge of such an account is to say what nonviolence is, which in turn requires saying something about violence. As the next chapter makes clear, giving a definition of violence that captures all instances of violence – while at the same time leaving out all instances of what isn't violence – is a difficult, and perhaps impossible task. The term violence is used in many ways and capturing those ways in a tidy definition may be a quixotic endeavor. Fortunately for us, we don't need to meet that challenge. Rather, the goal is the more limited one of asking what kind of violence nonviolence seeks to avoid. From there, we can turn to a positive conception of nonviolence. As I have mentioned, and as we will see in more detail, this conception revolves around ideas of respect and dignity.

From there, we turn to the different dynamics of nonviolence. There is a traditional view of how nonviolence is supposed to work that found its most coherent expression in Gandhi's thought and practice. This view requires a willingness to sacrifice oneself that appeals to the conscience of one's adversary. It is a view that remained associated with nonviolence through Martin Luther King's work. However, it is not the only way nonviolence can occur. Although there is no exhaustive categorization of different dynamics of nonviolence that can be given, we will examine several alternative dynamics to the Gandhian one.

The two chapters following that one are taken up with the task of investigating dignity and equality, respectively. The first concept has a long trajectory stretching back to the eighteenth-century philosopher Kant, and before that to earlier Catholic thought. However, my account makes use of that concept in a slightly different way from these earlier thinkers. In fact, there are two ways dignity appears in nonviolent activity. There is both the dignity of the adversary that is to be respected by nonviolent struggle and the dignity expressed by that struggle itself. Both of these ideas need to be investigated.

The interaction between these two forms of dignity leads to the idea of equality. Nonviolent struggle presupposes the equality of everyone: participants, adversaries, and bystanders. We need to understand what it is to presuppose such equality and how it appears in nonviolence. Then, of course, we should ask what the prospects are for nonviolence in our world. That will be the task of the concluding chapter.

One might ask here why we would need a specifically *philosophical* account of nonviolence? There are, as we will see, excellent histories of nonviolence as well as, more recently, sociological and political accounts of how and why nonviolence succeeds and sometimes fails. What would a philosophical approach add to these that would be helpful in reflecting upon nonviolence and acting nonviolently? After all, if we know the history and have a sense of what works and what doesn't, isn't that all we really need?

There is both a general and a specific answer that we can give to that question. The general answer concerns the philosophical value of reflecting on many things. To take time to ask what exactly it is one is doing or thinking, to subject it to critical scrutiny, is valuable on its own. Often, people are mistaken about various aspects of their lives – ethically, politically, epistemically, etc. – and philosophical reflection can bring out those mistakes and help address them. Alternatively, even where we are not mistaken, we may not know why it is that we are right. That is also worth knowing, so that our rightness is not a matter of brute luck.

More specifically with regard to nonviolence, there are questions that seem to require philosophical reflection before we can answer them. Most important among them are the questions of what nonviolence is and what gives it moral significance as a form of struggle. The answers to those questions are largely presupposed in the historical, political, and sociological accounts of nonviolence. Philosophical reflection, in contrast, does not presuppose those answers but seeks them. What this book hopes to do is provide a way of framing nonviolence that offers a plausible answer to the questions of what nonviolence is, why it works in the ways it does, and where its moral grounding lies. This reflection is not meant to supplant other studies of nonviolence. It cannot, by itself, give us examples of nonviolence the way the histories I rely on can. And it cannot give the kinds of accounts of success and failure that recent studies have so forcefully displayed. Rather than replacing these other works or lying below them as some sort of foundation, this philosophical reflection is an attempt to stand alongside them as another way of thinking about nonviolence, one with its own merits and limitations.

I suspect this work will not be the last word on the subject. Philosophy has so far largely neglected reflection on nonviolence. This is unfortunate in a violent world that calls out for – and more often we recognize, receives – nonviolent response. If I succeed only in provoking further thought and reflection among students of nonviolence and practitioners of philosophy, this will be enough. And if those students and practitioners can correct the inevitable flaws in my approach in order to offer something more adequate to the subject, this can only be to the good. Nonviolence is worthy of our attention and reflection, and this book will try to grapple within the limits of my ability with what it asks of us, recognizing that there is certainly more to be said.

Before proceeding, I should say a word about those limits of my ability. I am a philosopher who has organized and participated in nonviolent actions. In keeping with both my progressive political orientation and my role as a writer on political philosophy, I have tried to keep abreast of a number of political movements, both violent and nonviolent. I am not, however, a scholar of nonviolence. This should be emphasized, because among readers of this book there may be many who do not know that peace and nonviolence studies is a field – or better a set of fields – in which important work has been done. We should not think of peace or nonviolence studies as an intellectually barren area. As I hope this book will demonstrate, there are subtleties to the dynamics of peace and nonviolence that deserve much attention. I will not be able to address many of those subtleties, not only because they are beyond the ken of this book but also because I would be stepping into an area in which I would need far more knowledge than I have. The nonviolence studies – historical, sociological, and political – with which I deal here are recognized as central to the field; however, it should not be thought that they are exhaustive of it.

And with that, let us turn to the task itself.

2
What is Nonviolence?

Although the fortunes of nonviolent political action have risen in recent years, philosophy has not kept pace. This is unfortunate, because in academia at large that has been a minor explosion of publication about nonviolence, whether in recounting its history[1] or studying its character and effects.[2] In the following chapters, we will make use of this literature. Philosophy, however, has not followed this trend. There are no recent major treatises on nonviolence as such in the philosophical literature.[3] In fact, the most rigorous philosophical reflections on nonviolence remain those scattered across the writings of Martin Luther King, Jr, and Mohandas Gandhi and his followers.[4] (I will often use the term *nonviolence* as a shorter way to refer to nonviolent political action, although the term has also been used to refer to ways of living nonviolently that do not involve politics. These latter, however, are not our concern here.)

This chapter attempts to rectify this deficit by offering a philosophical characterization of nonviolence. The conceptual difficulties faced by such a task will make this chapter the most abstract of the book. We will need to consider a variety of positions, objections to them, reformulations, etc. But in the end we should have a working characterization of nonviolence that allows us to frame current discussions of the issue with some precision and clarity.

However, in order to understand nonviolence, we must start instead with a consideration of violence. This is not because nonviolence is simply the absence of violence. If it were, sleeping would be a nonviolent activity in the relevant sense. Nonviolent activity is nothing if not active. In fact, Gandhi ultimately rejected his own original term for non-violent activity – passive resistance – because of its overtones of inactivity, of undergoing rather than creating.[5] King, for his part, once wrote, "Nonviolent action, the Negro saw, was the way to supplement – not replace – the process of change through legal recourse. It was the way to divest himself of passivity without arraying himself in vindictive force."[6] However, one of the key characteristics of nonviolence is that it is *not violent*. In order to understand what nonviolence is, we need to understand what it rejects in rejecting violence.

This would seem to call for a definition of violence. However, things are more complicated than that. The term *violence* is used in many ways, not all of them having to do with political action. For instance, certain natural events are often characterized as violent. We think of earthquakes and tsunamis as violent, and even certain thunderstorms. Also, nonhuman animals often act violently toward one another. In rejecting violence, nonviolence does not address itself to predatory animal behavior or weather patterns. It is instead about something else.

Even when we turn to political references to violence, it is often difficult to get a grip on the term. One of the reasons for this is that the word *violence* is often used not just descriptively but also normatively. That is to say, it is used not only to describe certain behavior but also to offer implicit or explicit condemnation of it. As such, its parameters can extend fairly widely. To offer just one example from the recent literature, Slavoj Žižek's *Violence: Six Sideways Reflections* posits three types of violence: subjective, systemic, and symbolic. Subjective violence is violence as it is traditionally conceived, for example beating or killing someone. Systemic violence is "the often catastrophic consequences of the smooth functioning of our economic and political systems."[7] Symbolic violence, Žižek claims, is the violence performed in the very act of using language. "As Hegel was already well aware, there is something violent in the very symbolisation of a thing, which equals its mortification. This violence operates at several levels. Language simplifies the thing, reducing it to a single feature. It dismembers the thing, destroying its organic unity, treating its parts and properties as autonomous. It inserts the thing into a field of meaning which is ultimately external to it. When we name gold 'gold,' we violently extract a metal from its natural texture, investing into it our dreams of wealth, power, spiritual purity, and so on, which have nothing whatsoever to do with the immediate reality of gold."[8]

In his admittedly sideways reflections on violence, Žižek does not enlighten us as to the connection between someone's being beaten, being subject to an oppressive socio-political system, and being called a human. (For my own part, I am not convinced that just using language – as opposed, for instance, to using abusive language – shares enough with the previous two categories to be called violent. That seems, shall we say, casting the net a bit widely.) And if he were to do so, it is not clear that this would help us understand the character of nonviolence. While it is certainly true that nonviolent action rejects subjective violence and systemic violence (although we will shortly return to the complexities of that idea), it certainly does not reject what Žižek calls symbolic violence. In political organizing and political speech, language is used all the time. It is difficult to imagine organizing a nonviolent campaign without the use of language. Must nonviolence, then, be a matter of silence? Were the Estonian singers or the Occupy organizers engaged in some kind of activity that would place it on the same plane as the Soviet occupiers or even the bankers against whom Occupy protested? That seems a stretch.

How, then, are we to understand violence, or, more precisely, the violence that nonviolence must reject? To be sure, there are actions that almost everyone would characterize as violent, such as intentional physical harm directed at others. There are actions that almost nobody would label as violent, such as a prayer vigil in solidarity with a political prisoner. But what about the vast space in between the two? Can we set reasonable parameters of what is to be counted as violent, even if those parameters are a bit porous at the edges?

As a starting point, we can start with the philosopher Robert Audi's definition of violence. In his article "On the Meaning and Justification of Violence" he tries to offer a definition of all violence, not just the violence that nonviolence seeks to steer clear of. "Violence," he writes, "is the physical attack upon, or the vigorous physical abuse of, or vigorous physical struggle against, a person or animal; or the highly vigorous psychological abuse of, or the sharp, caustic psychological attack upon, a person or animal; or the highly vigorous or incendiary, or malicious and vigorous, destruction of or damaging of property or potential property."[9] The definition has three parts: one concerning physical violence, one concerning psychological violence, and one concerning violence to property. Let's lay aside the last part for the time being. We will return to it at the end of the chapter. For the moment, we can stick to the first two.

Certainly, a nonviolent movement will have to reject physical violence. That is a bottom line for nonviolent activity. Must it reject psychological violence as well? It would seem so. Imagine, for instance, Occupy protestors surrounding a Wall Street investor and engaging in humiliating personal chants. Or imagine in Tahrir Square protestors verbally tormenting the soldiers who monitored them, taunting them with insults and menacing threats to them or their families. There is something in these sorts of actions that seems to violate the spirit of nonviolence. After all, in nonviolence it is not the adversaries or the bystanders who are to be made vulnerable, but rather the protestors themselves. Part of the dignity (a term to which we will return) of nonviolent protest is that it seeks to elevate rather than diminish political action, and it does so in part by a willingness to undergo abuse rather than inflicting it on others. So it would seem that what Audi calls psychological violence would also be eschewed by a nonviolent campaign.

To be sure, the dividing line between psychological abuse and having a disturbing psychological effect is not always easy to draw. I was once involved in a campaign to end US financial aid to the contras in Nicaragua. The contras were a largely US creation that sought to overthrow the Marxist Sandinista government. It engaged in a campaign of ruthless terrorism and was widely condemned outside the USA. In one particular protest I was helping to organize, a leaflet was drafted that detailed some of the practices engaged in by the contras, for example cutting off women's breasts and throwing infants into the air and catching them on bayonets. Some of the other organizers argued that these leaflets were violent because of the abusive effect they would have on those bystanders who read them. While I did not share this opinion – in my view it was a characterization of violence rather than an act of it – the general point that the dividing line between calling attention to violence and engaging in psychological violence is elusive is worth bearing in mind.

Physical and psychological violence, as Audi has characterized them, are clearly anathema to nonviolent organizing and nonviolent campaigns. This does not mean, of course, that any campaign that engages in any physical or psychological violence at all is violent. Just as a swallow does not make a summer, a shove or a threat does not turn a nonviolent campaign into a violent one. Pure nonviolence is more an ideal than a description of certain campaigns. If we were to characterize only purely nonviolent campaigns as actually nonviolent, I suspect that no campaign would find itself in that category. It is probably most accurate to say that inasmuch as a campaign or an action is nonviolent, it seeks to reject physical and psychological violence.

However, there is another and more difficult question that we must face. It is the question of structural violence, or what Žižek calls systemic violence. This is the purported violence caused by an oppressive social, economic, and/or political structure. In fact, there are two questions here. First, is structural violence actually a form of violence? Second, in what ways, if any, should nonviolence abjure it? Audi, whose definition does not include the idea of structural violence, in fact rejects incorporating such an idea into his definition. He notes that "some people, especially some with a strongly Marxist bent, speak of violence where my definition would rule it out. Some speak of American society as doing violence to the Negro, referring to pervasive discrimination and exclusion...But it is difficult to see how we would gain by this. We would increase the risk of ambiguity and equivocation; and we would also increase the temptation, to which too many already succumb, of substituting a vague general term of disapproval for one which, like 'discriminatory hiring,' describes the specific grievance needing attention."[10]

The *locus classicus* of discussions of structural violence is Johan Galtung's "Violence, Peace, and Peace Research."[11] Published in 1969, it is the first sustained discussion of the issue. Galtung defines violence in general this way: *"violence is present when human beings are being influenced so that their actual somatic and mental realizations are below their potential realizations."*[12] Violence, then, "is that which increases the distance between the potential and the actual, and that which impedes the decrease of this distance."[13] Galtung offers as a consideration of violence the person who dies of tuberculosis. If such a person had contracted and then died from the disease in the eighteenth century, this would not be a case of violence. Since there was no cure for tuberculosis then, there was nothing that could decrease the distance from the actual (the disease) to the potential (the cure). However, since tuberculosis is treatable now, a person who contracts the disease but cannot get adequate treatment is the victim of violence. Their actual somatic realization is below their potential realization, while several centuries ago it would not have been.

The two types of violence that interest Galtung are personal violence and structural violence. "We shall refer to the type of violence where there is an actor that commits the violence as *personal* or *direct*, and to violence where there is no such actor as *structural* or *indirect*."[14] The latter occurs where "[t]he violence is built into the structure and shows up an unequal power and consequently as unequal life chances."[15] For instance, in an economic system where some have to work for others in order to avoid starvation, while those for whom they work are in no such danger, there is likely to be structural violence. This is because while there is nobody who is responsible for the situation as it is – assuming nobody involved in the system actually designed it – among its likely effects are that some workers are forced to take up menial or alienating labor in order to avoid starvation. Their somatic and mental realizations, then, would lie below their potential ones.

I have invoked the hedge word *likely* here, because it does not necessarily follow from the fact that this system exists that there would be structural violence. One can imagine such an economic system in which those for whom others work, call them the owners, are so concerned with the welfare of the workers that they ensure meaningful labor for everyone. In that case, actual and potential realizations could match, and there would be no structural violence. Thus, when Galtung uses the word *consequently* in describing structural violence, we should understand it as probabilistic rather than logical. Of course, there is a very high probability of such a consequence, given that almost all cases of such an economic system do have that consequence, but the conceptual distinction between the probable and the logical remains.

It might be objected that the economic system as I have described it, even with the kindly owners, would still constitute a situation of structural violence in Galtung's definition. Although the workers are offered meaningful work, it is still the case that they are subject to the whims of the owners. Should the owners decide that the workers' lives are too cushy or that their own offspring need a larger inheritance, their magnanimity would disappear. And since the workers' wellbeing is subject to that contingent magnanimity, and further, as is often the case, they recognize that subjection, their actual mental realization will fall below their potential mental realization. They will, in short, be insecure. That insecurity might, according to Galtung, be a form of structural violence.

This objection smuggles in an assumption that is not in the original example: the workers' awareness of the contingency of their situation. Without that awareness, and assuming the solicitous attitude of the owners, the workers might realize their potential. If they were to remain in a state of blissful ignorance – an ignorance perhaps reinforced through a history of owner decency – then it is imaginable that they would actualize their talents, enjoy their labors, and reap adequate fruits from those labors. It is, then, the assumption of an awareness of the contingency of their situation, combined with the (reasonable) assumption that that awareness leads to insecurity, and futhermore that that insecurity in turn leads to a failure to realize their potential, which gives the objection its force.

The force of the objection, however, does not only tell against the example I have used to illustrate the probabilistic character of the existence of violence in an economic system based on some working for others. It also raises an uncomfortable question to Galtung's definition of structural violence. What turns the economic situation I have described here from a nonviolent to a violent one is the workers' awareness of the contingency of the situation, and their reaction to that awareness. There is nothing violent in the situation until that awareness and its aftermath begin to settle in among the workers. But if that is what makes the situation violent, then in what sense would it be an example of *structural* violence? There is nothing in the structure of the situation itself that is oppressive. Rather, it is the subjective awareness of and reaction to the situation that, under Galtung's definition, makes it so. That awareness seems better understood as a *reaction to* the structure of the situation – and, more specifically, to the fragility of that structure – than as part of the structure itself.

What seems to be called for here is a more objective account of structural violence than the one Galtung has provided. His account, as it currently stands, seems to call structurally violent situations that we would hesitate to label as violent. Perhaps Galtung could amend his definition of violence in such a way as to rectify this difficulty. However, even if he could, there is another problem lying in wait for him. The philosopher C. A. J. Coady, in his article "The Idea of Violence," argues that Galtung's definition faces a difficulty that has nothing to do with subjective reactions.[16] Coady argues for a more restricted view of violence, one that would be closer to Galtung's view of personal violence as direct and perhaps intentional. On Coady's view, Galtung's definition is just too broad. "It seems to follow from it [Galtung's definition] that a young child is engaged in violence if its expression of its needs and desires is such that it makes its mother and/or father very tired, even if it is not in any ordinary sense 'a violent child' or even engaged in violent actions. Furthermore, I will be engaged in violence if, at your request, I give you a sleeping pill that will reduce your actual somatic and mental realisations well below their potential, at least for some hours."[17]

Neither of these counterexamples is concerned with structural violence. Rather, they are intended to show that the broader definition of violence Galtung posits, one on the basis of which he derives a view of structural violence, is itself wider than one can reasonably allow. Since one of the aims of the broad definition of violence is to allow for the recognition of the phenomenon of structural violence, then any narrowing of the definition risks leaving structural violence outside the reach of the term itself.

In arguing against Galtung's definition, Coady is not seeking to minimize concerns with social injustice. By restricting the definition of violence, he does not want to sideline the importance of the issues raised by what Galtung refers to as structural violence. Rather, he believes that assimilating social injustice to violence loses the normative specificity of social injustice itself, in much the same way Audi argues. "Both the existence of social injustice (i.e. 'structural violence') and restricted violence within, or between, communities are matters for moral concern but the way in which each relates to morality seems different … some acts of domestic violence may be morally legitimate, for example the violent restraint or hindrance of someone who is violently attacking someone else. By contrast, the idea that social injustice may be morally legitimate is more surprising."[18]

The problem with assimilating social injustice to violence, in Coady's view, is not only that the assimilation admits of counterexamples but also, and more deeply, that it leads to moral confusion. Violence, while morally problematic, is not necessarily morally wrong, as the case of violent defense against domestic abuse demonstrates. Social injustice, however, is always wrong. This difference is not just a definitional issue; it is also a normative one. By calling social injustice a form of violence, we fail to see it not only in its descriptive but also in its normative character: that is, we fail to see that it is always wrong.

Coady's conclusion is that we must stick with a more restricted definition of violence.[19] "Restricted definitions are typically those which concentrate upon positive interpersonal acts of force usually involving the infliction of physical injury."[20] He does not offer a definition of force, but does consider examples where there seems to be force without *physical* injury. Of particular interest is his attempt to assimilate psychological abuse to violence. He considers a tragic case, recounted originally by the journalist Newton Garver, in which the parents of a girl named Linda Ault punished her for adultery by having the girl take her dog to the desert. Coady quotes Garver quoting a newspaper account: "They [the parents] had the girl dig a shallow grave. Then Mrs Ault grasped the dog between her hands, and Mr Ault gave his daughter a .22 caliber pistol and told her to shoot the dog. Instead the girl put the pistol to her right temple and shot herself."[21]

For Coady, there is a justification for thinking of this kind of psychological abuse as involving violence. He writes, "if we consider a case in which someone skillfully works upon another's emotions and fears with a combination of words and deeds short of physical force, but with intentionally overpowering effects, then we may well feel that this is close enough to the physical model to be a case of violence."[22] He distinguishes this kind of case from that of structural violence, and worries about the slippage some people make between psychological and structural issues because both of them are, in his term, "impalpable."[23] He warns against this slippage, citing "the sheer immediacy and specificity of the pressure which is brought to bear upon the unfortunate girl with such overwhelming effects."[24]

However, there is a difficulty here involving impalpability, one that has insinuated itself into Coady's own treatment of psychological violence. Both when he defends the idea of psychological violence as violence and when he counsels against slippage from psychological to structural violence he refers to psychological violence in terms of its *effects*. What makes the act violent is not what the act *is* but what it *does*. Now one may refer to acts of physical violence as defined by their effects in the sense that, from the definition he uses, the "infliction of physical injury" is an effect of the act of force. However, in psychological violence the relation of act to effect is often not so easy to account for. In families with a history of abuse, the effects upon the offspring are often cumulative. The injury comes not simply from a single act of parental abuse, but from a repeated pattern of such abuse. Many parents, after all, lose their temper with their children in ways that they regret and subsequently seek to change. The real abuse and its effects often come not only from the degree of parental anger but also from its becoming a routine pattern of parent/child interaction.

Coady's treatment of the Ault case does not allow us to see this pattern as a form of psychological violence. He refers to the "sheer immediacy and the specificity of the pressure" to which the girl was subjected. In that way, he seeks to assimilate psychological violence to physical violence. However, the cost of assimilating this case in this way is that it precludes us from seeing repeated parental abuse that does its work over time, and perhaps with the same ultimately tragic effect, as a form of psychological violence. Further, it may have prevented us from seeing the Ault case aright. After all, if Linda Ault's parents were capable of such barbaric treatment of their daughter, in all likelihood this was not the first incident of parental abuse. Her suicide was likely the result not of this particular situation but of a pattern of parental brutality. It is difficult to imagine things otherwise. Suppose that the girl's parents were, up until this moment, caring and supportive of their daughter. Would the immediate turn to suicide have been likely in this case? More probable would have been confusion and a stunned disbelief, likely followed by a series of pleading questions that tried to reconcile what was happening at that moment with the previous trajectory of her relationship with her parents. That is to say, the effects of Ault's parents – the suicide – were likely not as immediate and specific to this incident as Coady believes.

And if they are not, is the case then no longer one of psychological violence? Would Linda Ault's parents' behavior only count as violent if what led to her suicide were the immediate effects of their actions right before it? This seems a counterintuitive position to take, although admittedly not an incoherent one. Coady himself seems to allow that psychological abuse, even in the Ault case, might not amount to violence when he writes of it that it was "clearly a dreadful act, and *perhaps* deserving of the name of violence."[25] However, this leads us to a dilemma. On the one hand, if we restrict the definition of violence to those acts with only an immediate relation to their effects, much of what seems to amount to psychological violence is no longer so. This is not an inconsistent position, but it does seem unduly arbitrary. Why is an immediate act of psychological abuse more violent than a series of acts that might have the same or even more profound effects upon their victim?

On the other hand, if we allow that nonimmediate effects can be determinative of violence, then have we not opened the door at least to the possibility of structural violence? Might it not be possible to consider other profound deleterious effects of certain situations to be violent ones? This is not to say that we can move directly from the admission of psychological violence to structural violence. Coady is correct to reject that move. Rather, it is to say that if we reject the idea of reducing the definition of violence to immediate effects, we cannot immediately rule the existence of structural violence out of court.

An objection might arise at this point to the direction I have taken. It might be pointed out that what physical and immediate psychological violence have in common is the idea that they are *intentional*. Regardless of the timing of effects of the violence, don't these types of behavior stem from an intention to harm that, as Galtung himself admits, is lacking in structural violence? However, psychological violence does not seem to require an intention to harm. In the case of Linda Ault's parents, there may have been no intention to harm her; rather, their intention, warped as their behavior was, could well have been to prevent her from the further harm that might come from repeated adultery. In fact, the regret expressed by Ault's father may testify to an intention like this. When he was interviewed after his daughter killed herself, he said, " 'I killed her. I killed her. It's just like I killed her myself.' "[26] To be sure, physical violence often seems to require an intention. Otherwise, cases of, for example, necessary surgery without anesthesia would be considered examples of violence. However, regardless of whether this is correct, there seems to be no intention to harm required in cases of psychological violence. In fact, one of the things that makes such violence so puzzling is that there often is no intention to harm, but rather an intention to improve, that is the motivation behind acts of psychological violence.[27]

Moreover, as Vittorio Bufacchi points out in his book *Violence and Social Justice*, some violence, even if not intended, can be foreseen. So for instance, if one drops smart bombs on an enemy, knowing that certain of those bombs are likely to go astray and kill civilians who are not intended as targets, that would seem to be an unintentional act of violence. Although Bufacchi wants to distance himself from the possibility of accidental violence – for him, violence must at least be something that is foreseeable – I think certain cases, like the Ault case, might count as forms of accidental violence as well.

If we admit that, in addition to physical and psychological violence, there might also be structural violence, this raises two questions. First, are all these forms of violence to be avoided by nonviolent action? Second, is there something in common with these different forms of violence that can bring them under a single umbrella, and in particular an umbrella that would allow us to label them all as violent?

The first question is easy to answer. Nonviolent action must avoid all three forms of violence. The first two we have already discussed. Structural violence must also be avoided. The reason for this is not far to seek. Structural violence is precisely the kind of thing that nonviolence seeks to confront and to change. Even if one rejects the assimilation of structural violence to violence in general, preferring instead to label it, with Coady, social injustice, it is still the object of nonviolent resistance. The Egyptians in Tahrir Square sought to end the violence (or social injustice) of the Mubarak regime; the Estonians sought to end the violence of the Soviet occupation; many of those involved in the Occupy movement sought to end the structural violence associated with an economy that allows some to flourish while many struggle to cobble together a decent existence. All of these are examples where structural violence (or, once again, social injustice) is involved, even if, as in the first two cases, physical and psychological violence were also being resisted.

A more classic example of nonviolence resisting structural violence is in the US Civil Rights movement. The marches, sit-ins, Freedom Rides, etc. were attempts to use nonviolent methods in order to resist structures that left African-Americans living in the South disenfranchised. To be sure, there was plenty of physical and psychological violence involved in the South's segregation, from lynching to humiliation. But the fundamental problem was structural. African-Americans were part of a social, political, and economic system in which they were rendered second-class citizens, without the right to vote, to eat where they liked, to sit where they liked on public transportation, to educate themselves at good schools and universities, to obtain good jobs, etc. This system was one of structural violence against African-Americans. It was precisely this structural violence which was to be resisted. Therefore, to engage in a form of structural violence would have been to encourage something the Civil Rights movement was seeking to end, even if in another form.

Nonviolent action and nonviolent campaigns, then, avoid physical, psychological, and structural violence. Returning to the second question, then, is there something these three forms of violence have in common that would bring them together under a single category, that of violence? In his book on violence and social justice, Bufacchi offers a definition of violence that he hopes will capture the range of different types of violence. It is broader than Audi's, because it seeks to include what I have called here structural violence. "An act of violence occurs when the integrity or unity of a subject (person or animal) or object (property) is being intentionally or unintentionally violated, as a result of an action or an omission. The violation may occur at the physical or psychological level, through physical or psychological means. A violation of integrity will usually result in the subject being harmed or injured, or the object being destroyed or damaged."[28]

On this definition, the possibility of structural violence is opened up by the inclusion not only of acts but also of omissions and also of the inclusion of unintentional as well as intentional actions and omissions, although, as we have seen, for Bufacchi those actions must have foreseeable consequences, not just accidental ones. So suppose, for instance, in an act of foreseeable but unintended violence, a banker forecloses on someone's home, knowing but not intending that doing so will result in that person's having a mental breakdown, then one has engaged in an act of violence. We can push the example a little further, however. Suppose that I support the existence of banks that have policies of closing on people's homes, and suppose it is generally known that such policies have effects of violating people's psychological integrity. Then I am still engaged in violence, and we would call such violence structural violence.

The burden of Bufacchi's analysis of violence is carried by the word *integrity*. Bufacchi says that, "In defining violence as the violation of integrity, the term integrity is used here in a strictly nonphilosophical sense, meaning wholeness or intactness."[29] In characterizing integrity this way, he notes a debt to an earlier author, Gerald MacCallum, who also wrote of violence as the violation of integrity. In "What is Wrong with Violence," MacCallum ties integrity not only to the wholeness of one's body but also to the autonomy of the person. "The aspect of autonomy generally most at issue in discussions of the integrity of persons is that concerned with the self-determination of what happens to one."[30] Integrity, then, is a matter of retaining a whole self that can decide what is to happen to it and what is not.

In looking at violence this way, we cannot, of course, think of "the self-determination of what happens to me" in too broad a sense. For instance, there is no violence done to me if someone comes up to me and starts speaking to me without my permission, or hands me a book I have not asked for. The example MacCallum considers is far more invasive – that of amputation. So the sense of "me" here in what happens to me has to be a deeper one, which MacCallum recognizes causes difficulties in sorting things out. Bufacchi tries to capture the idea with the images of wholeness and intactness. If someone starts speaking to me unbidden or hands me a book, my wholeness remains intact in a way that it does not when I am shot or psychologically abused, perhaps through public humiliation. I am also not left intact if I cannot provide for myself in an adequate way, which allows for the possibility of structural violence.

We should bear in mind here that both MacCallum and Bufacchi, like Audi, Galtung, and Coady, are seeking to define violence per se, not simply the violence that nonviolence rejects. They are thus characterizing a broader notion. One might raise questions about whether their definition, as a definition of the entirety of violence, isn't too broad. For instance, suppose one divorces a spouse who is emotionally dependent on one, and suppose the divorce has years of psychologically deleterious effects. For instance, the divorced spouse suffers from long-term depression as a result of the divorce, has trouble relating to others, and perhaps performs poorly at work for many months. This would seem to constitute a violation of integrity in Bufacchi's sense. However, I suspect we would hesitate to call the divorce an act of violence.[31] The problem here is that integrity can be undermined in many ways. Not all of those ways are properly categorized as violence.

Bufacchi might defend his definition against the divorce example by saying that while the divorce might have *undermined* the spouse's integrity, it did not *violate* it. This, of course, would call for a reflection on what constitutes a violation as opposed to an undermining. Bufacchi offers us tools for this reflection when he says that violence can happen through acts or omissions, but that those acts or omissions, even if not intentional, must at least involve foreseeable consequences to a person's integrity. As an example, he offers the case of one's grandmother dying of hypothermia that could have been foreseen while the grandson and his spouse are on vacation in Venice, commenting that "all suitably qualified impartial rational persons would agree that there is no moral difference between the positive action of killing my grandmother and the omitting action of going on holiday with the same consequences."[32]

However, it is unclear that this clarification would help in the divorce case. Would the divorcing of the spouse, even if the effects could have been foreseen, constitute an act of violence? It seems not. The problem here remains one of breadth. The violations Bufacchi discusses, because they can be foreseeable omissions, seem to open the door to characterizing more as violence than most of us would be comfortable to countenance. To be sure, his definition is narrower than Galtung's, but as a definition of violence it may yet be too broad.

The divorce case, however, is directed against the adequacy of Bufacchi's definition as one that seeks to characterize *all* of violence. Our immediate question is narrower. Even if the definition will not stand as a definition of violence, might it characterize the type or types of violence that are rejected by nonviolent actions and campaigns? After all, nonviolent action does not count either vacations or divorce among its tactics, so might the definition serve as the background against which to view nonviolence?

Thinking about violence in terms of integrity, and integrity in terms of the "self-determination of what happens to me" is attractive. It seems to capture the idea that a nonviolent action or campaign must display some respect for both its adversaries and bystanders. However, it also seems to imply that a nonviolent campaign cannot be coercive. Coercion, after all, violates autonomy in the sense that it prevents people from determining what happens to them, and in fact prevents them from determining their future. When one is coerced, one is blocked from acting as one would otherwise want to act. One's preferred course of action is made impossible, or at least very difficult. Coercive action is, then, a violation of autonomy.

Is nonviolence coercive? It often is, and in fact often is meant to be, a point that we will take up at length in the following chapter. For the moment, consider, as an example, the Montgomery bus boycott of 1955, which happened in the wake of Rosa Parks' being arrested for refusing to move to the back of the public bus as African-Americans were required to do in the South at that time. The boycott was designed to put economic pressure on the Montgomery bus companies and also upon the public institutions that allowed those companies to segregate passengers. It was not merely a call to conscience, but a pressure placed upon the companies and state institutions. And, in fact, it succeeded precisely through coercion when a federal court ordered the buses to be de-segregated.

Was the boycott coercive? The point of the boycott was not only to display the egregious discrimination of the practice of making African-Americans ride in the back of the bus, although that was certainly one goal. It was also to force the Montgomery bus system to integrate its buses, or at least partially integrate them. And in this it was successful. The US Supreme Court declared the segregated bus system unconstitutional, and the system was forced to integrate.

To be sure, not all nonviolence is coercive, or is meant to be. The Occupy movement, while seeking to call attention to the unfair distribution of wealth in the USA, did not have any mechanism for coercing change. However, the occupation of Tahrir Square arguably did. Its defiance of the Mubarak regime was intended not simply to call attention to his rule but to end it through noncooperation. Nonviolent action, then, can certainly be coercive, and therefore a violation of autonomy in the sense MacCallum discusses.[33]

Is there another way to think about violence as the violation of integrity Bufacchi proposes that can recognize that nonviolent action can be coercive while still rejecting violence? I believe there is. In order to capture it, I would like to use the word *dignity*.

In his book *Dignity*, Michael Rosen traces a history of the term.[34] He finds three major strands in the history of the concept, and then proposes a fourth. The first is associated with the history of Catholicism and is a matter of seeing dignity as the inherent value of persons, one's elevated status as a human being. The second is the familiar Kantian notion of dignity as an intrinsic value associated with the possession of reason and therefore bearers of the moral law. The third is dignity as a way of behaving: dignity as acting in a dignified manner. Finally, "the third strand examined, the idea of dignity as behavior that is dignified, reveals a fourth: a perspective on dignity from which to treat someone with dignity is to treat them with respect. Instead of respecting dignity by respecting a set of fundamental rights, dignity requires respectfulness. Taken in this way, the right to have one's dignity respected is one particular right – albeit a very important one – rather than something that acts as the foundation for rights in general."[35]

It is, I believe, dignity in this fourth sense described by Rosen that is what nonviolence seeks to display, and its violation that is the particular kind of violence that nonviolence seeks to avoid. Moreover, it is perhaps the violation of dignity in this sense that Bufacchi gestures at with the idea that violence violates the integrity of another. As Robert Holmes argues, "Persons are preeminently worthy of respect, and each person has a claim upon those whose conduct may affect him to be treated in ways which do not diminish him. To deprive him of his freedom, degrade him, or destroy his confidence are all ways of doing the latter and all are accomplishable without resort to physical violence. Indeed, most of them can be effected through the subtlest forms of personal and social interaction, inasmuch as it is in these areas that people are often the most vulnerable."[36]

However, we need to specify the idea further. What is it to fail to treat another with respect?

It is, broadly, to fail to treat that other as having a life to lead, one that, while not immune to coercion, must at least be taken seriously as one goes about one's own actions. Conversely, to respect another is to take that fact seriously. Violations of integrity, then, in Bufacchi's sense, will be failures to respect the dignity of others in the sense of acting in ways that fail to take into account the fact that others have their lives to lead and are not simply there to serve one's own ends.

This idea of respecting that others have a life to lead is a bit vague, but perhaps not hopelessly so. We have a sense of what it is in general to lead a human life: to engage in projects and relationships that unfold over time; to be aware of one's death in a way that affects how one sees the arc of one's life; to have biological needs like food, shelter, and sleep; to have basic psychological needs like care and a sense of attachment to one's surroundings. In addition, we are developing a sense of the lives and needs of various nonhuman animals that can help us structure nonviolent relationships with them.

This is not to say that every life, human or otherwise, is led in exactly the same way. People have various ways of leading their lives, and we who interact with them are often aware to one extent or another of these varieties. To respect that specific others have a life to lead does not require that we defer to every desire they possess. If it were then, once again, nonviolent coercion would be impossible. As nonviolent theorist Barbara Deming says in her seminal essay "On Revolution and Equilibrium," where she argues that nonviolent "equilibrium" requires aggression or self-assertion as well as nonviolence, "It is quite possible to frustrate another's action without doing him injury ... To impose upon another man's freedom to kill, or his freedom to help others kill, is not to violate his person in a fundamental way."[37] (One way to understand the task of this chapter would be that of working out what might be meant by the term "injury" invoked by Deming.) Instead, such respect is a matter of recognizing that even if certain desires of others are frustrated by nonviolent action, those others must be left with a route that allows them to continue to engage in meaningful projects without fear of psychological or physical abuse or without lacking access to basic goods.

This view of respecting the dignity of others contrasts with a more subjective view like MacCallum's, in which autonomy is grounded in the individual's desire. The reason for this is that if we allow for such subjective grounding, then nonviolence coercion would by definition be violent. The existence of coercion would be a violation of autonomy, and as such would be violent. It also, I hope, explicates the idea of integrity that Bufacchi endorses, saying more about the kinds of wholeness or intactness that is required if integrity is not to be violated.

As a side note, I should mention in passing that this view of dignity has much in common with Kant's view, with one important change, a point to which we will return in the fourth chapter. While it concurs with Kant that dignity must be respected, and sees disrespect as often involving using another as a means to one's end, it does not ground dignity in reason. For Kant, respecting the dignity of others is a matter of respecting their capacity for reason, and thus for acting in accordance with what he thinks of as the moral law – which is purely a matter of reason. The view I am proposing here is concerned less with rationality than with the idea that lives have shapes or trajectories, and that respecting them involves a recognition of that, even if not always a deferral to the specific shape or trajectory one has chosen. This does not mean that rationality does not count or is irrelevant to such respect. The formation of projects and relationships often involves rationality, even if not Kant's pure rationality. However, by widening the scope of recognition from reason to the shape of one's life, this view allows us both to take in more of human life – as well as nonhuman life – as relevant for consideration in thinking about nonviolent action.

This scope also allows us to recognize what the three forms of violence we have considered here – physical, psychological, and structural – have in common. Physical violence certainly does not recognize that the victim has a life to lead. It treats the other simply as an object for one's anger or one's purposes. Generally, it does this in a twofold manner. First, its form of coercion takes place as a disrespect of the other. Rather than recognizing that, even if the other must be coerced, that coercion should take place in a way that allows one the maximum latitude to be able to continue on the paths of his or her life, physical violence interferes with that life without regard for that latitude. Second, physical violence in many cultures is humiliating and produces psychological scars. It has the effect of making it difficult for its victim to navigate through the world at all. For the victim of physical violence, the world becomes an insecure place, one in which it is difficult to engage in one's projects without a sense of fear.

This, of course, is not true of all physical violence. Physical violence associated with sports like boxing or rugby, for example, would not seem to undermine that ability of the object of violence to lead his or her life. In general, it seems that physical violence voluntarily undergone would not have the effects I have just described here – although there may be exceptions. (And there may be those who would claim that what I am calling violence in sports, because it is voluntarily undergone, is not actually violent, a claim that we need not settle here.) Our goal, recall, is not to offer an account of all violence, but only the violence that nonviolence seeks to avoid. In an act or campaign of nonviolence, adversaries and bystanders are not in a situation in which they would volunteer for violence, and so the violence – if it is indeed violence – associated with certain sports or other activities does not arise.

One might try to press the question and ask whether the view on offer here would allow violence in some strange case in which an adversary would undergo it voluntarily, or even seek it. Perhaps such a case would arise when the adversary would be trying to provoke violence, and violence against himself or herself, in order to discredit a nonviolent campaign. This would seem not to involve a disrespect for the dignity of the other. In fact, oddly enough, it would seem to promote the projects of the victim of violence. Could one then say that the view here would, contrary to how nonviolence works, allow for physical violence?

I believe the answer to this question is no. This is not for the simple reason that the person provoked doesn't know that the provocation is occurring and therefore is disrespecting the adversary. *Expressing* disrespect for the dignity of another need not be a matter of *intending* such disrespect – an issue we will return to below in the discussion of structural violence. If this is right, the problem here does not lie in the intention to disrespect the adversary, but elsewhere. Rather, the problem is more indirect. By allowing oneself to be provoked into physical violence, one's actions suggest that disrespect for the dignity of others is not to be avoided in the course of nonviolent action. While this may not, through the peculiar set of circumstances in which it arises, be a form of disrespect for the particular victim of physical violence, inasmuch as it countenances physical violence toward adversaries, it winds up disrespecting those other adversaries who have not sought to provoke violence.

Another complication that arises when considering physical violence is the vexed issue of violent self-defense. Is it possible to defend oneself with violence against another while still respecting the dignity of another? Can one attack another physically and at the same time take seriously the fact that they have a life to lead? If so, then my proposal would be inadequate, since nonviolent action requires that one not physically attack others, even in self-defense.

I am tempted to say here that any form of violent self-defense involves a significant diminishing of respect for the dignity of the one attacked. This is not to say that such self-defense would not be justifiable. Whether an act is nonviolent and whether it is justifiable are two different things – unless, of course, one is a pacifist. My claim here is not that one would not be justified in the disrespect shown for the other in violent self-defense, only that violent self-defense does display that disrespect. To have to defend oneself violently is to be put in a situation where one can only retain one's own physical integrity by disrespecting the other. That is the unfortunate but inevitable situation that such self-defense puts one in, and what makes it so vexed. To be sure, there are different degrees of violent self-defense, and to defend oneself with the minimal degree of force required to fend off attack may still display some degree of respect for the other. However, the fact that one has to, or feels one has to, attack another physically in order to defend oneself seems to require at least a suspension of the respect nonviolence would require for the dignity of others as I have described it here.

If we turn to the second form of violence, psychological violence and abuse, we can see that, based on our discussion of physical violence, the matter is simple. Psychological violence is always a matter of disrespect for the dignity of the other, because it is always a matter of violating the dignity of the other, interfering with the fact that the other has a life to lead. In this way, although nonviolence has focused on avoiding physical violence, it may be that psychological violence is even more contrary to the character of a nonviolence movement than physical violence.

This is not to say that there are no difficulties associated with the concept of psychological violence. For instance, while it is rarely difficult to know when an instance of physical violence has taken place, it can be more elusive to assess cases of psychological violence. This is particularly true in a nonviolent campaign, which often involves coercion. How, one might ask, might the line between nonviolent coercion and psychological violence be drawn? This is an important question, but, I suspect, one that can only be answered in the context of a particular nonviolent campaign. There seems to me to be no bright philosophical line that can be drawn between the two. Acting nonviolently requires being attuned to the issue, seeking to confront one's adversaries in a way that does not deny them the dignity of leading meaningful lives. Here it is a matter of judgment and sensitivity more than having criteria, even the loose criteria we are considering here.

Structural violence is the most complicated of the three, since there is no direct relationship between the actor and the object of violence. In fact, the "actor" might seem to be a structure rather than a person. However, while that is not mistaken, it is not the entirety of the story. It would be more precise to say that in structural violence certain social and political structures are directly violent while certain people are indirectly violent by contributing to those structures. The sense in which the structures are directly violent stems from the situation those structures put people in, a situation where people are treated as though their lives were not important either because they were expendable or because they were just means to the improvement of the lives of others. A classic example here would be slavery, which, in addition to its physical and psychological violence, is a system in which slaves are treated as property rather than as persons with their own lives and their own projects and relationships.

Another example is the American South under Jim Crow. While there were certainly many acts of physical and psychological violence, what was most pervasive was a particular order in which African-Americans were treated, as the term says, like second-class citizens. In this case, second-class citizenship included the denial of a decent education, lack of access to professional jobs, exclusion from better housing and neighborhoods, denial of voting rights, a humiliating requirement to defer to whites on buses, while walking on the street, etc. The social, political, and legal structures in the Jim Crow South were arranged so that African-Americans were treated not as independent people who had lives to lead but instead as means to further the lives of Southern whites.

One might ask whether the very idea of a structure that oppresses people would be counterintuitive. It is easier to see how a person might be violent toward another than to see how a structure might. What is a structure that it can do violence toward a person? We should not, however, think of structures as spooky kinds of entities. A structure is nothing more than a particular arrangement of social, political, cultural, and economic practices. It is, in some sense, a way of life. Just as we say that a certain family atmosphere is oppressive, meaning not that there is this thing called an atmosphere which oppresses people but instead that the patterns of family behavior make it difficult for people to be at ease, so a violent structure is an arrangement of practices that make it difficult for certain people to conduct their lives as though they mattered.

It is in this way that structures can be violent. However, people in those structures can be violent as well, only more indirectly. By contributing to Jim Crow, through paying taxes to racist governmental structures or by voting for segregationist politicians or simply by living uncritically in the system itself, many whites were indirectly violent toward their fellow African-Americans. This is not to say that there weren't acts of direct personal violence. There were plenty of those. Lynchings, for instance, were numerous in the Jim Crow South. Rather, in addition to those acts – which helped keep the structural violence in place – there were many people who contributed to the structural violence of the South by going about their lives in a way that contributed to others' not being able adequately to do so.

One of the implications of this is that people can be violent toward others not only indirectly but also unintentionally. We saw this in the case of psychological abuse, but that would be a more rare phenomenon. In structural violence, people are often unaware of the contribution they make to the disrespect of others' dignity. In fact, in situations of structural violence there is often a lot of self-deception that prevents people from seeing clearly their contribution to the violence. This can occur in many ways: through physical segregation into separate neighborhoods, ideological excuse ("those people are not capable of our achievements"), illusions of camaraderie ("some of my best friends are Negroes"), or a simple refusal to look clearly at the situation to which one is contributing. The self-deception would not have to be in place were people not vulnerable to feeling a sense of responsibility for the structural violence to which they contribute. In fact, one might say that it is often because people are situated (or situate themselves) to contribute unintentionally to a situation of structural violence that it can continue to exist.

There is a further question that we might ask here, one that takes us beyond Bufacchi's claim that violence can be done not simply intentionally but also foreseeably: can one commit violence accidentally? After all, if people can contribute to violence without intending to, isn't it possible that they can do so without any sense that that's what they are doing?

Consider a simple example. Imagine that there is a nonviolent sit-in blocking a road that leads to a military installation where training to invade another country is taking place. Unbeknown to the protestors, an ambulance is trying to get through this road but is blocked by the traffic, and the patient dies as a result of the blocked road. Would this, then, turn a nonviolent protest into a violent one?

One can see the implications of this for structural violence. If the answer to this question is no, then, as Bufacchi argues, what is called structural violence must be at least reasonably foreseeable by those who contribute to it in order to be violence at all. Alternatively, if the answer is yes, then many nonviolent protests might actually be violent through no fault of the protestors. In fact, whether they are violent or not is largely not in their control. Protests can be planned to be nonviolent under all kinds of circumstances, and yet could become violent through some unforeseeable contingency.

Frankly, I am not sure what to say about this. My own intuitions are conflicted. On the one hand, the idea that non-violent protests can become labeled as violent purely through a strange accident seems mistaken. On the other hand, it also seems to me that contributing to structural violence can be done without even reasonable foreseeability. People who are not in a position to recognize the contributions their actions make toward the debilitation of others' lives may still be contributing to that debilitation in a way that seems like structural violence. And, on the third hand, I am not sure that there is some argument to make structural violence, while still violence, into a special category of violence that would allow accidental contributions while nonviolent protests would not.

Fortunately, it is not necessary to answer this question in order to define what nonviolence *seeks* to achieve. What is crucial to nonviolence is that it abjures all forms of violence: physical, psychological, and structural. The first two are obvious, and the third should follow close behind. Nonvio-lent actions and campaigns are dedicated, in one way or another, toward allowing people to construct meaningful lives for themselves. If nonviolence does so in a way that contributes to structural violence, then it is undermining the very spirit out of which it operates. Nonviolence does not concern the dignity of *this* or *that* group of people (or animals). It concerns the dignity of all people (and relevant animals). If nonviolence rejects violence against one's adversaries, surely it must reject violence against bystanders and others who could be affected by its actions. Otherwise put, if the adver-saries against whom nonviolent struggle is waged are to be respected in the fact of their having lives to lead, so must everyone else who could be affected by that struggle. There-fore, nonviolence must seek to avoid structural as well as physical and psychological violence.

I should note before offering a more specific definition of nonviolence that the view of structural violence offered here is narrower than that offered by Galtung. For him, recall that "violence is present when human beings are being influenced so that their actual somatic and mental realizations are below their potential realizations," and violence "is that which increases the distance between the potential and the actual, and that which impedes the decrease of this distance." This allows for a very wide definition of violence, one whose difficulties Coady calls attention to, for example with the son who tires his father or the person who asks for sleeping pills knowing that they will inhibit performance. The definition of violence offered here – or, more precisely, the characterization of the type of violence that nonviolence seeks to avoid – is narrower than Galtung's definition. It does not concern the blocking of individual potential so much as the broader failure to recognize that others have a life to lead. Structural violence, then, which is the central point of contention between Galtung and Coady, is not subject to the objections Coady raises, although he would probably continue to prefer the term social injustice to refer to what I have called structural violence. This preference is in itself only a semantic difference, as long as we recognize what it is that nonviolence is seeking to avoid. My own preference and argument for that preference are based on the commonality shared by the structural, the physical, and the psychological, and the semantic cleanliness of contrasting these as matters of violence with acts and campaigns that are considered to be *non*violent.

With this characterization of the violence rejected by nonviolence in hand, we are ready to turn directly to a delineation of nonviolence itself. As I mentioned at the beginning of the chapter, we cannot define nonviolence solely in negative terms as the absence of violence. If nonviolence were solely the absence of violence, then I would be acting nonviolently when I was sleeping or taking a shower. Nonviolence instead is a type of activity, or better a range of different activities that seek to challenge a current set of arrangements, whether political or economic or social. Because of this, we may define nonviolence as *political, economic, or social activity that challenges or resists a current political, economic, or social arrangement while respecting the dignity (in the sense defined above) of its participants, adversaries and others.*

There are several points worth noting about this definition. First, it is indifferent between a nonviolent act and a nonviolent campaign. I have used both of these terms throughout the chapter. We should not think of campaigns as simply series of acts, although they are that as well. For campaigns, if conducted at all well, are organized and coordinated affairs. The sociologists Erica Chenoweth and Maria Stephan, whose book *Why Civil Resistance Works* is a detailed study of a century's worth of disobedience (we will return to their work in the following chapter), define a campaign as "a series of observable, continual acts in pursuit of a political objective."[38] The acts that comprise them therefore have an internal relationship to one another. For simplicity's sake, I will refer to both simply as nonviolence, although the term more often refers to campaigns and not simply individual actions.

Second, nonviolence is not restricted to the political realm, unless we define that realm very broadly (a definition to which I have no objection). Economic boycotts may be examples of nonviolence, depending on how they are carried out. We will discuss such boycotts in the following chapter when we consider the dynamics of nonviolence. Challenges to certain social arrangements can also be instances of nonviolence. For instance, in 1924 there was a campaign (to which we will return) to challenge forbidding Indian "untouchables" from using a road that passed directly by the Vykom Temple in the state of Travancore in the southwest of India. This campaign involved "untouchables" and their supporters using the road and allowing themselves to be beaten by the Brahmins who objected to it, and later by the police who barricaded the road. In addition, the protestors stood in front of the barricade during the monsoon season, often in water up to their shoulders. Their eventual victory was a successful challenge to the social caste system that characterized Hindu culture in India and that was a particular object of Gandhi's opposition.[39]

Finally, the phrase *respecting the dignity of its participants, adversaries, and others*, while seeking to capture the discussion of violence that preceded it, glosses the question of whether there can be such a phenomenon as accidental violence in a nonviolent action or campaign. As I noted, I am unsure how to resolve that issue, and that uncertainty is reflected in the definition of nonviolence.

To some, the definition offered here might seem too broad. For example, it would seem that someone who writes a letter to their Congressperson challenging that person's stand on a particular political issue would be engaged in an act of nonviolence. However, that's not how we normally think of nonviolence, and it is certainly not the kind of nonviolence that we saw in the previous chapter. How can we compare a letter to a Congressperson with the collective sonorous resistance of the Estonian people or the courageous gathering of protestors in Tahrir Square? On the surface, they seem to be entirely different species of activity.

To be sure, we often think of nonviolence as something grander and more majestic than such letter-writing. But that does not mean that we need to exclude activities like these from the category of nonviolence. In fact, letter-writing is often part of the strategy of a nonviolent campaign, alongside the more visible activities of occupation and public protest. Although we might say that an individual writing a letter to a Congressperson who is not part of a larger campaign is not engaged in the kind of sustained collective campaigns of nonviolence that we are studying here, that does not mean that such an activity is not itself a nonviolent one. At worst, we might say that it is not a particularly interesting example of nonviolence.

Others might think of this definition of nonviolence as too broad in another way. Suppose, for instance, that a nonviolent demonstration blocks the entrance to a corporate headquarters of a company that manufactures nuclear weapons. (When I lived in Pittsburgh, we once memorialized Hiroshima Day by staging a die-in at Rockwell headquarters that effectively blocked the building's entrance for a short period.) Since such a blockade would hinder people from going about their jobs, would it not display a disrespect for people's having lives to lead?

It would not. Recall that there is a distinction between recognizing that people have lives to lead and allowing them to do what they like. Nonviolence is compatible with certain kinds of coercion. If such a blockage put people in a position where they lost their jobs, that might be a matter of disrespect. This would rarely happen, however, particularly at a corporate headquarters. Even if the blockade were over a longer period, if there were a loss of jobs that would likely be the result of corporate firings rather than the demonstrator's actions. This would be in contrast to blocking a small, independent grocery store where a long-term blockade would likely result in the loss of livelihood for those who worked in it, and indeed in many cases with the further consequence that it would be difficult for those working in the store to find other employment. (Demonstrating in front of such a store, for instance to protest against its selling of Israeli goods in violation of the Boycott, Divestment, and Sanctions campaign, would not be violent, since it would not prevent people from engaging in their livelihood.)

One might also ask whether nonviolence must abjure not only violence but also *threats* of violence. Take, for instance, the moment in the Estonian campaign in which the Soviet troops surrounded the television tower and the Estonian policeman, Jüri Joost, threatened to release Freon that would kill himself and the troops as well. The threat was successful in keeping the troops temporarily at bay, but was it an act of nonviolence? It might be argued that it was, since nobody was harmed physically, psychologically, or of course structurally. However, there seems to be something disingenuous about allowing nonviolence to threaten harm, even when it doesn't employ it. After all, don't threats of violence rely for their efficacy on the very violence that nonviolence is expected to reject?

There are, I think, two ways of addressing this issue, but they have the same result that nonviolence must reject not only violence but also threats of violence. First, one might make the case that threats of violence are in fact a form of the kind of violence that nonviolence seeks to avoid, since they don't actually respect the dignity of others in the sense defined above. In threatening violence one appeals to the same concerns – an inability to carry on a human life – that violence does, and so there is no interesting distinction between performing violence and threatening to. Alternatively, it might be conceded that threats of violence are not actual violence, but that such threats violate the spirit if not the letter of the violence that nonviolence seeks to avoid. If nonviolence necessitates respecting the dignity of others, appealing to a technical way of avoiding charges of violence does not seem to be in keeping with what is sought in such respect.

Turning our attention to traditional nonviolent campaigns, we immediately run across an issue that our definition must address: the distinction between what is commonly called strategic or practical nonviolence and principled nonviolence. The sociologist Kurt Schock describes the difference this way: "Pragmatic nonviolence is characterized by a commitment to methods of nonviolent action due to their perceived effectiveness, a view of means and ends as potentially separable, a perception of the conflict as a struggle of incompatible interests, an attempt to inflict nonphysical pressure upon the opponent during the course of the struggle to undermine the opponent's power, and an absence of nonviolence as a way of life. Alternatively, principled nonviolence is characterized by a commitment to methods of nonviolent actions for ethical reasons, a view of means and ends as inseparable, a perception of the conflict as a problem shared with the opponent, and acceptance of suffering during the struggle in order to convert the views of the opponent, and a holistic view of nonviolence as a way of life."[40]

There are specifically Gandhian elements in this distinction that are not entirely necessarily to it, especially in regard to the difference between incompatibility and sharing and the necessity of conversion over undermining (a necessity that Gandhi himself was ambivalent about), but otherwise the distinction is captured precisely in this summary. Roughly, we might think of the difference between practical and principled nonviolence to be one of the motivation behind the actions that a nonviolent campaign takes, rather than a difference in the actions themselves, although that motivation could at times lead to different actions. Advocates of practical nonviolence see nonviolence in terms of *success*: a nonviolent campaign is more likely to achieve the goals of the movement than a violent one. This could be for any number of reasons. It might be that the superior military or police forces of the adversary would render violent resistance futile. Perhaps the campaigners would prefer a violent form of resistance – it would be quicker, for instance – but, given the military strength of the adversary, it is just not feasible. Or it might be that, in order for the campaign to succeed, it needs the support of the broader public, and violent resistance is likely to diminish that support. As many nonviolent movements provide evidence – from Gandhi's campaigns in India to the US Civil Rights movement to the Arab Spring protests in Tahrir Square – nonviolence often garners the sympathy of those not directly involved, and such garnering can be crucial to the success of a campaign. Or yet again, it might be that there are weaknesses in the adversary's structure that would be better exploited through a nonviolent campaign. It could be, for instance, that the economic structure is heavily dependent on the production of particular items or the exportation of particular resources, and organizing a strike among the workers in those areas is more likely to be successful than the resort to violent resistance.

In all of these scenarios, the choice of nonviolence is solely a strategic one. There is no commitment to the dignity of the adversary, only to the promise of nonviolence to attain the ends sought. By contrast, principled nonviolence requires taking the dignity of the adversary (and bystanders) seriously on its own terms. To use Kant's language, it requires seeing the adversary as an end in itself rather than simply as a means to one's own ends. Principled nonviolence would not countenance the resort to violence even if it were more effective. Violence isn't an acceptable means of struggle for the advocates of such a position; it is never on the table for discussion alongside other, nonviolent means of resistance.

Principled nonviolence is very close to pacifism, and probably in most cases coincides with it. It is difficult to imagine a pacifist who would not endorse principled nonviolence, or a practitioner of principle nonviolence who was not also a pacifist. However, one could imagine a practical pacifism, just as there is practical nonviolence. The difference between a practical pacifism and practical nonviolence would be that the former would argue that violence is never more effective for challenging particular political, economic, or social arrangements, while the latter only holds that position for the particular situation in which struggle is taking place. In this case the practical pacifist would have no particular regard for the dignity of the adversary in any struggle, but only a strategic commitment to respect that dignity for the sake of achieving desired ends. To be sure, this seems an unlikely position, and I am not aware of anyone who holds it. However, unlikelihood is not impossibility; a practical pacifism – in essence a generalized practical nonviolence – is a view of nonviolence that can be endorsed without incoherence.

Having made the distinction between practical and principled nonviolence, however, we should ask what it amounts to in the course of nonviolent struggle. I think that, as a matter of challenge and resistance, there is less to separate the two than the differences just drawn might lead us to believe. Assuming that a campaign is in fact nonviolent, what would be the difference between its being one in which the campaigners actually respected the dignity of its adversaries and one in which the participants only *pretended* to do so, or somehow did so only as long as the campaign lasted? I suspect there is little to differentiate such movements. Whether one respects the dignity of others because it enhances one's ability to achieve one's ends or does so because one believes it is the right thing to do will matter little to whether a campaign is nonviolent or not. It is the structure of the campaign – or its actions – rather than the motivation behind them that decides whether a campaign is nonviolent or not.

One might object here that participants in a campaign of nonviolence that are only practically committed to it are more likely to turn toward violence than those who are committed by principle. This is undoubtedly true. However, it does not affect the character of the campaign – or its actions – as nonviolent. The fact that a particular campaign might be exchanged for another one under the right conditions does not change the nature of that campaign itself. A nonviolent campaign – one that respects the dignity of others – does not become violent merely by the fact that its participants would turn toward violence under circumstances other than the ones that currently obtain.

This might make it seem that the motives of those who participate in nonviolence are entirely irrelevant to the character of a nonviolent campaign. It is only what is done and not done that matters. And if that's true, then what do we make of the word *respect*, which seems to imply some kind of motive?

However, motives are not entirely irrelevant to a campaign of nonviolence. To commit to nonviolence is to commit to a way of acting toward others, even if one finds the actions of those others abhorrent. In doing so, it commits to whatever motives are necessary to be able to act that way. Put another way, one must train oneself to be nonviolent, especially where one's instincts might lead one toward violence. That involves learning to act on the basis of certain motives. Although I may be motivated to disrespect another because of his or her or their heinous behavior, if I am to engage in nonviolence I cannot act on that motive. I must instead act on the motive that recognizes, however reluctantly, that the other has a life to lead and is not simply there for my purposes.

That is all the motive of respect for the dignity of others requires. It does not require that I love, or even like, my adversary (although the rhetoric of love has often been invoked in reflections of nonviolence). For all this respect requires, I may detest the adversary. However, if I am to act nonviolently it cannot be out of the detesting that I act. If one were to ask of nonviolent actions that they be motivated out of a respect that views another more positively than this, it would be asking more than nonviolence requires. To be sure, there are views of nonviolence that do ask more than I have posited here as necessary for respect. However, the goal here is not to understand any particular nonviolent orientation, but rather what all nonviolence has in common.

However, even if a *feeling* of respect for the other is not necessary for respecting their dignity, acting in accordance with nonviolence might itself have effects on the participants, effects that might move at least some participants from a more practical to a more principled embrace of nonviolence. The reason for this is not far to seek. When one disciplines oneself to behave a certain way, one can internalize the way of life associated with that kind of behavior. If, for instance, I train myself to look at another person's face while criticizing them in order to help refrain from a natural habit of being callous, it is likely that over time I will in fact become less callous. Our actions are not only a product of our motives; our motives are also a product of our actions.[41] Because of this, extensive participation in nonviolence may lead one toward a more nonviolent orientation generally. This more nonviolent orientation is, of course, principled nonviolence. It may be unlikely that someone who becomes oriented in this way would ever embrace a position of strict principled nonviolence. However, we need not think of the difference between practical and principled nonviolence as a binary one. One can be more or less principled in one's nonviolence, just as one can be more or less principled in one's vegetarianism or one's religious commitments.

Before turning to the various dynamics of nonviolence, it is worth pausing over an issue that has been left aside since the initial discussion: whether one can be violent toward property. Recall that in Audi's definition of violence, among the ways violence can occur is through "the highly vigorous or incendiary, or malicious and vigorous, destruction of or damaging of property or potential property." And for Bufacchi, "an act of violence occurs when the integrity or unity of a subject (person or animal) or object (property) is being intentionally or unintentionally violated, as a result of an action or an omission." Audi and Bufacchi, of course, are trying to define violence generally, not only the violence that nonviolence seeks to avoid. That is not our task. We do not need to answer the question of whether destruction of property is violent, only whether it is the type of violence nonviolence must avoid.

The framework for answering this question is the one we have already developed. Does the destruction of property fail to respect the dignity of others? Does it fail to recognize that others have lives to lead? If we put the matter this way, the answer is, it depends on the particular property being destroyed.

Property is not merely stuff. It is not simply inert matter that happens to lie in one place rather than another. *Property*, as Marx taught, is a social relationship. Property involves belongingness, and to belong to someone is a status that can happen only through being recognized as belonging by the rules of a particular society. Moreover, that recognition can take many forms. We in the West are used to thinking of property mostly as private: property is a matter of belonging to a particular someone. But property can be jointly owned as well, or it can be owned by the people and administered through the state, or it can be commonly owned without a particular administrator. What this means for our purposes is that when property is destroyed, the question of whether that constitutes violence that must be avoided requires, among other things, knowing whose property it is.

Suppose, for instance, that in the course of a public demonstration a group destroys the statue of a dictator that the group is trying to overthrow. The statue, if it is the property of anyone, belongs to the dictator. In this case, there is no or maybe no disrespect for dignity of the dictator. If the group merely wishes to show that it no longer fears the dictator's power over them, then such destruction would seem to be in keeping with nonviolence as I have described it. Alternatively, if the destruction is meant to symbolize the desire to destroy the dictator himself, then that would be a violence in conflict with respect for the dignity of the other. Of course, the activity of destruction itself would likely offer a clue as to which alternative is being chosen. If the statue is merely toppled and then carted off, that would likely indicate the former. On the other hand, if the statue is trampled, and kicked and generally treated as one would treat a human being that one is beating, that would more likely indicate the latter.

During the alter-globalization movement of the late 1990s and early 2000s, there were a number of cases where demonstrators who called themselves the Black Bloc threw rocks through the windows of corporate property such as Starbucks. Most other demonstrators found this activity objectionable. One reason they did so was that the activity seemed to paint a picture of the demonstrators as an unruly mob. Therefore, it was unhelpful in getting across the demonstration's message. This seems to me to be right on target. But we might raise a question distinct from that one: was the throwing of rocks through the windows of corporate buildings an instance of violence that nonviolence should seek to avoid, independent of whether it is a helpful tactic?

Here again, the answer is, it depends. For instance, to throw rocks through the windows of a Starbucks coffee house would likely affect the ability of people to work there. In particular, they might be afraid of further personal attacks, and that would certainly affect their ability to lead their lives. In general, throwing rocks through windows might seem to have that effect. However, if the rocks were thrown through the window of a corporate headquarters on a Saturday afternoon when nobody was working and it was clear that the incident would not be repeated, that would perhaps be a different story. When it comes to rock-throwing, there would have to be a very specific set of circumstances in which it would not induce the kind of fear that is a form of disrespect for the dignity of others. Whether in reality that could be done is difficult to say.

We now have a concept of nonviolence in hand. This concept can offer guidance in understanding how nonviolence works. In the following chapter, we will look at the different dynamics of nonviolence. As it turns out, nonviolent campaigns are of many varieties, and these different varieties have their own dynamics. In this way, resistance to particular political, economic, or social arrangements can occur that respect the dignity of others while challenging them in very different ways.

3
Dynamics of Nonviolence

There is a tendency, as we noted in the previous chapter, to see nonviolence as passive rather than active. This seems to be the implication of the term with which nonviolence is often associated: passive resistance. Gandhi was leery of the term passive resistance, preferring his own term satyagraha. The term satyagraha, he wrote in 1921, "was coined in South Africa to distinguish the nonviolent resistance of the Indians of South Africa from contemporary 'passive resistance' of the suffragettes and others. It is not conceived as a weapon of the weak."[1] Nonviolence as a type of political campaign is rather a form of struggle – or better, a set of forms of struggle – characterized by respect for the dignity of the other. Those forms of struggle must be creative, in the sense that they cannot rely on conventional military intervention even when, as is often the case, they are aligned against an adversary that itself is armed and prepared to use military force.

One can see why nonviolence might be thought to be a "weapon of the weak." The idea behind this thought is that many who are oppressed, particularly in a despotic state, do not have access to military weapons, or at least to enough of them to pose a credible challenge to the powers they resist. Therefore, they turn to nonviolence as an alternative form of struggle, one that is not preferred but instead resorted to when better means are unavailable. This chapter will try to show that such a thought is mistaken. The dynamics of nonviolence are not a lesser set of means but often a better one, notwithstanding well-known failed nonviolent campaigns like the one in Tiananmen Square. Nonviolence is often a better means not only in its moral aspect but also in its political consequences. Nonviolence should not be seen as a way to struggle against a superior force with inferior means, but instead as a way to shift the ground of struggle so that superior military force becomes irrelevant or even a disadvantage.

We can give some initial impetus for this view by citing the success of nonviolent campaigns over the course of the past century. Erica Chenoweth and Maria Stephan, in a recent important comparative study of violent and nonviolent movements, *Why Civil Resistance Works: The Strategic Logic of Nonviolent Conflict*, compared 323 violent and nonviolent struggles over the period from 1900 to 2006. They did not seek to incorporate all forms of nonviolent struggle – that would have made the study unwieldy – but instead confined their work to anti-regime, anti-occupation, and secession movements. They report, "The most striking finding is that between 1900 and 2006, nonviolent resistance campaigns were nearly twice as likely to achieve full or partial success as their violent counterparts... in the case of anti-regime resistance campaigns, the use of nonviolent strategy has greatly enhance the likelihood of success. Among campaigns with territorial objectives, like anti-occupation or self-determination, nonviolent campaigns also have a slight advantage."[2] Only in secession movements, where the population of part of a territory seeks to form its own polity divorced from the rest of the territory, do violent campaigns do any better than nonviolent ones. However, neither has been very successful. While nonviolent campaigns over the studied time period did not succeed at all, violent campaigns only succeeded ten percent of the time.

These findings do not cohere well with either the idea that nonviolence is a weapon of the weak or the thought that it is a strategy for those who lack a better, that is, military, option. It might also be a surprising finding, given how little nonviolent conflict appears in public view. There may be many reasons for this. One of them is certainly that nonviolent conflict, although it often captures the imagination of those who participate in it, does not so capture the media. Images of nonviolent struggle – except when they are met with violent repression – are not the stuff of media concern. They rarely provide the striking images that are likely to elicit television coverage. Aside from iconic images like those of water cannons blasting civil rights protestors in Birmingham, Alabama in 1963 or of a lone Chinese citizen confronting a tank headed to Tiananmen Square in 1988 or the fictional presentation of Gandhi's salt march chronicled in Richard Attenborough's 1982 film *Gandhi*, nonviolence rarely occupies the media – and therefore our collective consciousness – to the degree that violent conflict does.

If nonviolent resistance, although less often followed, is more often successful, what makes it so? What are the dynamics of nonviolence that render it so fruitful as a set of means of struggle? The object of this chapter is to canvass different approaches to nonviolent struggle, to see how nonviolence works. As we will soon discover, there isn't a single form of nonviolent struggle but instead several. These forms share important commonalities aside from their being nonviolent. But they are not reducible to one another and they are not derived from a single formula.

Perhaps the most influential model of a dynamic of nonviolence is the one traceable back to Gandhi. By "traceable back" I mean that Gandhi himself did not offer a systematic account of nonviolence, although, as Joan Bondurant shows in *The Conquest of Violence: The Gandhian Philosophy of Conflict*, a systematic account can be drawn from his dispersed writings. However, before we come to grips with Gandhi's view, we should recognize that nonviolence did not begin with Gandhi's efforts in South Africa and then in India in the early part of the twentieth century. There were commitments to nonviolence as a form of living or resisting among early Christians, Quakers, the Diggers, abolitionists, and others stretching back two thousand years before Gandhi articulated his vision of satyagraha.[3] However, it was left to Gandhi, and particularly his leadership in the Indian movement for independence from Britain, to give shape to what is often thought to be *the* model of nonviolent action.

We might think of satyagraha as normatively anchored in two principles: truth and what in Hindi is called *ahimsa*, refusal to harm. These two are related. The term satyagraha can be translated as "soul-force," but also, and probably preferably, as "truth-force." As Gandhi wrote, "The word *Satya* (Truth) is derived from *Sat*, which means 'being.' Nothing is or exists in reality except Truth."[4] (Sometimes Gandhi equated the idea of Truth with that of God.) Truth, then, as the ultimate reality, is what ought to be strived for. However, it is not so easy to tell who has understood the Truth. Reasonable people differ in their views of what is real and what reality is. Because we are limited and fallible beings, none of us can be sure of the correctness of our views.

This is where *ahimsa* becomes important. It is one thing to press one's own views, to make a case for them, and even to engage in confrontation with those who refuse to recognize them. It is another thing altogether, however, to do violence to those who refuse to recognize what one takes to be the Truth. Violence is not confrontation; it is suppression. Those who engage in violence are not simply trying to get others to recognize the Truth. They are instead seeking to eliminate those who refuse to ratify what they take to be the Truth. This constitutes a refusal to come to terms with the limited and uncertain grip that one can have on the Truth. It is to take oneself to be something other than what one is, to see oneself as a deity rather than a human being. In order to avoid this mistake, one has to cling to *ahimsa*, to refuse to do violence to others. "*Ahimsa* and Truth," Gandhi says, "are so intertwined that it is practically impossible to disentangle and separate them. They are like two sides of a coin, or rather of a smooth unstamped metallic disc. Who can say, which is the obverse, and which is the reverse? Nevertheless, *ahimsa* is always the means; Truth is the end...If we take care of the means, we are bound to reach the end sooner or later."[5]

If this was all there was to Gandhian nonviolence, we would be left to wonder whether it is anything more than just a harmless doctrine of respect for one another, or even a form of passivity where each has his own truth and none can dictate to another. However, to abjure violence does not require one to refrain from confronting others. Moreover, that confrontation can involve a clash between two views of the Truth, even if at least one side refuses violence. And one can go further. As Bondurant points out in her study of Gandhi, "Despite the protestations of a few followers of Gandhi that satyagraha is always persuasive and never coercive the method does contain a positive element of coercion. Noncooperation, boycott, strike – all of these tools which may be used in satyagraha involve an element of compulsion which may effect a change on the part of an opponent which was initially contrary to his will."[6] But if this is so, it leaves us with an uncomfortable question. How can one reconcile *ahimsa* with coercive nonviolence? Won't any attempt to impose one's views on another beyond mere persuasion be a form of violence against another? And if we try to reconcile the two by restricting *ahimsa* solely to a refusal to commit *physical* violence, aren't we simply failing to recognize the other forms of violence we encountered in the previous chapter?

In short, how can nonviolence, especially in its Gandhian form, be at once coercive and indeed not violent?

The answer to this question must involve a dynamic that brings someone who disagrees with one's view of the Truth to come to recognize it through a pressure that does not violate his or her dignity. The first step in applying this pressure is one that can most easily be seen to preserve the dignity of the adversary: persuasion. Persuasion was, for both Gandhi and later Martin Luther King, a necessary first step in any nonviolent campaign. As Bondurant writes, "Satyagraha allows for several stages of winning over an opponent. The first stage is characterized by persuasion through reason."[7] King, in describing the nonviolent campaign he helped conduct in Birmingham, insisted that "In any nonviolent campaign there are four basic steps: collection of the facts to determine whether any injustices exist; negotiation; self-purification; and direct action."[8] Of course, if persuasion were always effective, there would be no need for a theory or strategy of nonviolence. Instead there would just be a theory of rational political persuasion.

It might seem that the attempt to persuade an adversary, particularly one who already enjoys the benefits of power, would be naive. However, there are two reasons it is a necessary stage in a nonviolent campaign, particularly a campaign based on Gandhian principles. First, it is in keeping with

Gandhi's insistence that nobody has a claim to privileged access to the Truth. One must always admit the possibility that one is mistaken. That is why *ahimsa* is a necessary means to truth. So one must approach the adversary recognizing that it is possible that the adversary will reveal an aspect of the situation of which one has been ignorant and which might change one's mind. This does not mean that one has to be reticent in pressing one's own view. As King noted, preceding negotiation is "collection of the facts." A nonviolent campaign cannot be initiated on the basis of ignorance. Negotiation or persuasion, then, are not matters of approaching the adversary in order to hear what it has to say. They are instead active engagements seeking to convert the other to one's viewpoint. But they must remain *open* engagements, allowing one to hear the adversary even as one speaks to it.

This can only happen where the adversary is treated as worth hearing, as another person or group of persons with a viewpoint that, while different from one's own, is not inferior *by virtue of being different*. In other words, while the adversary may be wrong, this does not stem merely from the fact that their view differs from one's own. To think that would be to ascribe an inferiority not only to the adversary's position, but to the adversary himself or herself or themselves. It would be to violate the dignity of the adversary. This is the second reason for beginning a nonviolent campaign with persuasion or negotiation before turning to more coercive methods.

What happens when, as is often the case, persuasion fails? How are adversaries to be coerced while their dignity remains respected? In Gandhi's view, the answer can be summed up in one word: suffering. After persuasion through reason, Bondurant writes, "The subsequent stages enter the realm of persuasion through suffering wherein the satyagrahi attempts to dramatize the issues at stake and to get through to the opponent's unprejudiced judgment so that he may willingly come again onto a level where he may be persuaded through rational argument."[9] Or, as the political scientist Dustin Howes articulates it with regard to a violent adversary, "Gandhi offered a particular form of satyagraha as a direct response to violence. Tapas, or self-suffering involves doing precisely what Clausewitz says is impossible: refusing to submit one's will and yet also refusing to respond to violence with violence."[10]

Suffering, for Gandhi, is the key to coercion without violence. How might suffering work? One suggestion would be that suffering would move the adversaries to relent on their position out of pity for the nonviolent campaigners. This, however, would be mistaken, for two reasons. First, many people in positions of power either do not see or can easily justify to themselves the existence of the suffering of others. There is no lack of defenses of inequality, even radical inequality; and there is no lack of ways of blaming the poor for their poverty or the unfortunate for their misfortune. It might be that public suffering would make the misfortune more vivid to the adversary. However, it is not clear that vividness would be enough to motivate changes that might result in the loss of privilege for the adversary.

The second reason is, from a Gandhian standpoint, more important. Pity is not the same thing as embrace of the Truth. If the *ahimsa* is supposed to allow the adversary access to the Truth, then it should operate by bringing the individual to see where it is wrong. Pity is, in a way, the opposite of that. It moves one away from understanding in the face of the vividness of immediate pain. Recall that for Gandhi nonviolence is not a weapon of the weak but of the strong. It would be contrary to Gandhi's nonviolence to base a solution to the problems it raises through a response that emphasizes weakness rather than strength. If suffering is the key to Gandhi's nonviolence, then, it must operate in some other way.

This other way was first captured in a term coined by the social philosopher Richard Gregg: moral jiu-jitsu. In his 1934 book, written in the midst of the movement for Indian independence from Britain, Gregg describes the moral jiu-jitsu of nonviolence this way:

> The nonviolence and good will of the victim act in the same way that the lack of physical opposition by the user of physical jiu-jitsu does, causing the attacker to lose his moral balance. He suddenly and unexpectedly loses the moral support which the usual violent resistance of most victims would render him. He plunges forward, as it were, into a new world of values. He feels insecure because of the novelty of

the situation and his ignorance of how to handle it ... The user of nonviolent resistance, knowing what he is doing and having a more creative purpose, keeps his moral balance. He uses the leverage of a superior wisdom to subdue the rough direct force of his opponent.[11]

Nearly thirty years later, King describes the American Civil Rights movement in much the same terms:

> When, for decades, you have been able to make a man com-promise his manhood by threatening him with a cruel and unjust punishment, and when suddenly he turns upon you and says: "Punish me. I do not deserve it. But because I do not deserve it, I will accept it so that the world will know that I am right and you are wrong," you hardly know what to do. You feel defeated and secretly ashamed. You know that this man is as good a man as you are; that from some mysterious force he has found the courage and conviction to meet physi-cal force with soul force.[12]

Gregg offers several reasons for this moral jiu-jitsu of nonvio-lence: a loss of self-confidence in the adversary, a new-found respect (as opposed to pity) for the opponent, the moral censure of onlookers, and an openness that derives from being in an unfamiliar situation. It is worth examining moral jiu-jitsu more closely, in order to see how coercion can occur without disrespecting the dignity of the adversary. Let us look first at its general characteristics and then consider an example from the Indian independence movement.

Nonviolent resistance begins where persuasion and nego-tiation end. In one way or another – through demonstrations, sit-ins, marches, occupations, or other tactics – people pub-licly disobey or challenge the current social and political order. Such activity can be ignored by the adversary, and sometimes is. However, under at least two conditions it isn't: either when the adversary brooks no opposition or when the opposition catches the public eye and becomes a source of increasing discontent. Then it is usually repressed. In more authoritarian or totalitarian regimes, this repression is gener-ally violent. Such violence has been on display in many of the cases we have already looked at: Estonia, the Philippines, the Mubarak regime in Egypt, Britain's occupation of India, and the American Civil Rights Movement. There were even tinges of it in clearing out Zuccotti Square at the end of New York Occupy.

In nonviolent resistance, the moment of repression leads not to an abandonment of the movement nor to a turn to retaliatory violence, but instead to a steadfast engagement in the movement itself. This engagement does not flee from the suffering imposed by the adversary. Quite the opposite. It takes it on as part of its struggle. It recognizes, and allows others to recognize, that it is willing to suffer for the sake of its goals. In Gandhi's terms, the members of the campaign are willing to suffer for the sake of the Truth.

This, in turn, becomes the moment of moral jiu-jitsu. When the adversary is revealed as violent, its members are seen not as interested in justice but only in their own self-interests. They are revealed as those who would not seek the Truth but rather to suppress it in favor of protecting their privileged status (or having their police or military protect it for them). And not only are they revealed to be this way to others; they are also revealed – or can be revealed – to be this way to themselves. This is what King means when he writes: "Nonviolent direct action seeks to create such a crisis and foster such a tension that a community which has constantly refused to negotiate is forced to confront the issue...we must see the need for nonviolent gadflies to create the kind of tension in society that will help men rise from the dark depths of prejudice and racism to the majestic heights of understanding and brotherhood."[13]

We might think of moral jiu-jitsu in contrast to what is often called the cycle of violence. In the latter, violence begets more violence, since each act of violence seems to call out for retaliation. You harm someone I care about, so I must harm you or someone you care about. There is something deep in human nature or at least human history that tempts reactions of violence as a response to violence. What the moral jiu-jitsu of nonviolence does is turn the arrow of reaction back from the potential object to the actor. Where violent activity affects someone who is close to the harmed person by focusing his or her attention on the harmer, moral jiu-jitsu turns attention back to oneself. It is as though a successful act of nonviolence makes the adversary rather than the nonviolent actor more visible to the adversary itself; rather than seeing the nonviolent actor, one sees oneself as if in a mirror. In this way, the cycle of violence characteristic of violent resistance is not only blunted, but in a way reversed.

Moral jiu-jitsu, or what the nonviolent theorist Gene Sharp calls political jiu-jitsu, does not affect only the adversary. As Sharp writes, "Political jiu-jitsu operates among three broad groups: (1) uncommitted third parties, whether on the local scene or the world level, (2) the opponent's usual supporters, and (3) the general grievance group."[14] The moral crisis appears for group 2, the opponent or adversary. However, the suffering of the nonviolent campaign also has effects on outside witnesses and the group itself. For outside witnesses, the suffering of the campaigners calls attention to their goals. It does not do so through pity, but rather through another mechanism: through steadfastness in the face of the suffering endured, the demands of the campaign become more difficult to ignore. What might once have been a conflict distant from one's own experience is placed before one in a more immediate way. And because the suffering is endured actively rather than undergone passively, the reaction of outsiders is generally one more of admiration than pity. This allows them to take seriously the goals of the group, to look upon them with a sympathetic eye.

Within what Sharp calls the "grievance group" the admiration for those who withstand suffering provides a model and perhaps a spur to join the campaign. Seeing others suffer on one's behalf can be motivating, pulling those among the oppressed who have stood on the sidelines to become members of the resistance themselves. This happens not through threat or through guilt, but rather through a sympathy with and esteem for those who are standing up in one's own name.

What is to be emphasized here is that, in a Gandhian dynamic of nonviolent resistance, the moral jiu-jitsu – the rebounding back of violence against the adversary in the form of moral condemnation and crisis – is neither simply pity for those who suffer nor blind admiration, but rather the opening onto the issues in play that such suffering creates, what Gandhi would call an opening onto the Truth. The situation as one of injustice is revealed to all, including members of the adversary. This allows for the final moment in the Gandhian dynamic: conversion. "Satyagraha," Gandhi writes, "is a process of conversion. The reformers, I am sure, do not seek to force their views upon the community; they strive to touch its heart."[15]

Conversion occurs when the adversary comes to see the rightness of the position of a nonviolent campaign. What the suffering of the campaigners reveals is not their vulnerability, but their access to Truth. And through their suffering, and the pressure applied by those who support them, the adversary can also be brought to see the Truth. What was conveniently ignored previously can no longer be ignored. One is brought face to face with an aspect of the Truth that one might have otherwise been able to deceive oneself into believing did not exist. That aspect of the Truth is in general one's participation in injustice against others: exploiting them, not offering them the proper respect as fellow human beings, participating in social or political structures that dominate them, preventing them from obtaining the resources with which to construct a meaningful life, marginalizing them from community engagement, and so on.

This does not mean that the adversary does not also have some access to the Truth, an access that could be recognized in the unfolding of a nonviolent campaign. As Bondurant notes, "What results from the dialectical process of conflict of opposite positions as acted upon by satyagraha, is a synthesis, not a compromise. The satyagrahi is never prepared to yield any position which he holds to be the Truth. He is, however, prepared – and this is essential – to be persuaded by his opponent that the opponent's position is the true, or more nearly true, position."[16]

In Gandhian nonviolence, then, the dignity of the adversary is respected. The adversary is coerced into recognizing the Truth, but not through a means that fails to respect that he or she or they have lives to lead. In the previous chapter, I described what is to be respected this way: *We have a sense of what it is in general to lead a human life: to engage in projects and relationships that unfold over time; to be aware of one's death in a way that affects how one sees the arc of one's life; to have biological needs like food, shelter, and sleep; to have basic psychological needs like care and a sense of attachment to one's surroundings.* In Gandhian nonviolence, even when it coerces the adversary into recognizing an aspect of the Truth that had been previously ignored, that dignity of the other is always respected. This is one of the reasons conversion is so important to him. Conversion welcomes the other into the Truth rather than forcing the adversary to bow to something that still seems foreign or false.

There are several campaigns in India that more or less follow the Gandhian dynamic of nonviolent conversion. Among them the 1924–5 campaign to open the Vykom Temple Road to untouchables, mentioned briefly in the previous chapter, is perhaps the most illustrative.[17] (Some would say the more famous Salt March would serve just as well; however, it involves important elements of accommodation discussed below. We will return to the Salt March in the fifth chapter.) In India, the traditional Hindu caste system rendered people subject to the caste into which they were born. The most elevated class was that of the *Brahmins*, which were followed by three other castes. At the bottom of the social scale, excluded from any caste, were the *Dalits* or "untouchables." They were prohibited from direct contact with the Brahmins because it was thought that such contact would sully the Brahmins with their impurity. In this case, the Dalits were prohibited from using the road that passes by the Vykom Temple at Travancore, in southern India. This prohibition made it difficult for the Dalits to conduct their lives, since they had to take roundabout routes to go to and from their homes to work.

The Vykom Temple Road campaign was not initiated by Gandhi, but he later supported, advised, and through negotiations participated in it. Its beginnings were simple. After unsuccessful negotiations with the Brahmin community for access to the road, and after prayer and preparation, the Dalits engaged in marches across the Vykom Temple Road. They were met by violence, beaten by Brahmins and arrested by police. Rather than retaliate, however, the campaigners merely kept their marches. Those who were arrested were replaced, and those who were beaten returned to march.

Eventually, the jails were filled and the police adopted another tactic: they blocked the road. In response, the campaign placed people in front of the barricades. They did not try to storm or even go around the barricades. As Gandhi wrote in opposition to a proposal to go over the barricades, "For scaling barricades is open violence. If you may scale barricades, why not break open temple doors and even pierce through temple walls? How are volunteers to pierce through a row of policemen except by using force?"[18] Instead, they placed themselves before the barricades and remained there in three-hour shifts.

As the monsoon season approached, the road became flooded and the police staffed the barricades in boats. The protestors did not abandon their vigil, however, often standing for several hours in water that was up to their shoulders. During this period, Gandhi visited Travancore and negotiated a removal of the barricades. One might have expected at this point that the campaign would be over. However, it was not. The campaign decided that, although the barricades were gone, it was not yet time for them to use the road. This is because the Brahmins were not yet persuaded that the Dalits *deserved* to walk on the Vykom Temple Road. After several months of prayers and negotiation, the Brahmins announced that, "We cannot any longer resist the prayers that have been made to us, and we are ready to receive the untouchables."[19] This campaign had ramifications across India, allowing the Dalits to obtain access to roads and temples that had been previously barred to them.

The dynamic of the Vykom Temple Road campaign follows the Gandhian script closely. After the failure of persuasion, a nonviolent campaign that involves suffering is initiated. The suffering, in turn, leads to a moral jiu-jitsu in which those who are violent are confronted with the intertwining of the steadfastness of the campaigners and their own injustice. This opens the way for a conversion experience that recognizes the Truth of the nonviolent campaign. While there is coercion that occurs, it is a moral coercion, one that forces the adversary to come to terms with an injustice that has previously been ignored. The dignity of the adversary is not violated in this coercion.

Is this dynamic of nonviolence – the traditional Gandhian one – the only way to respect the dignity of the adversary? If so, and if respecting dignity is the hallmark of a nonviolent campaign, then very few campaigns would actually be nonviolent. In fact, of the four campaigns with which this book started, it is unclear that any of them would qualify as a strictly Gandhian campaign. The Soviets withdrew from Estonia, but were not converted. Mubarak was forced to abandon his office, but it is unlikely that he – or, as time has shown, the military – were converted to the goals of those who occupied Tahrir Square. While the Occupiers in New York and elsewhere were persuasive to many in the country who were not in the one percent, there was no mass conversion (or perhaps even a single conversion) of Wall Street executives or monied interests in abandoning support for increasingly inegalitarian distributions of wealth.

The one case where conversion did play a role, but only a partial role, was in the Philippines. There many among the military who were sent to the square to disperse the protestors were converted by their steadfastness. One commander of a helicopter team who had been listening to descriptions of the demonstration on the radio recalled that the announcer "was giving a blow-by-blow account of what was going on. It made me sad."[20] Although he was sent to attack the defectors, he instead flew his helicopters to the rebel base. However, although many who witnessed the demonstrations were converted, others were not, in particular Ferdinand Marcos. He left the Philippines, but without ever acknowledging the injustice of his regime.

If we are to recognize the protests in Estonia, the Philippines, Egypt, New York, and elsewhere as nonviolent, and yet concede that at least the first three were (or in the case of Occupy sought to be) coercive in their way, then we must also recognize that not all nonviolence occurs in accordance with the Gandhian script. Although there is a nobility to Gandhian nonviolence, there must be other forms of nonviolence that have their effects in other ways. In particular, we must recognize that not all nonviolence is a matter of conversion.

Bondurant points the way in this direction by claiming that beyond the stages of negotiation and suffering, there is a third stage to which a Gandhian politics might have to resort. "Finally," she writes, "if persuasion by reason or by suffering does not succeed, the satyagrahi may resort to nonviolent coercion characterized by such tools as noncooperation or civil disobedience."[21] It is, of course, possible that noncooperation can lead to conversion. In fact, in the Vykom Temple

Road campaign, the participants engaged in noncooperation when, in violation of law, they marched along the forbidden road. However, in this case the major elements in persuading the Brahmins may not have been the noncooperation but instead the willingness to suffer in front of the police barricades combined with the subsequent refusal to use the road until the Brahmins gave their blessing. In cases of noncooperation, it may be that the adversary is converted. But as we have seen with the examples at the beginning of the book, the results instead may be something less than conversion. The theorist Gene Sharp widens the concept of nonviolence precisely in this direction.

Gene Sharp's three-volume *The Politics of Nonviolent Action*, published in 1973, remains for many the touchstone of nonviolent theory and action. It is a monumental tome, displaying not only a subtle grasp of nonviolence but also an encyclopedic view of the history of nonviolent resistance. Those who have studied political philosophy know that no serious political theorist can afford to ignore John Rawls' 1971 work *A Theory of Justice*. I would argue that the same holds true for Sharp's work in nonviolence and peace studies. The first volume of *The Politics of Nonviolent Action* offers his view of the theoretical structure underlying nonviolent action. The second volume covers different methods of nonviolent action, listing, describing, and exemplifying not less than 248 different kinds of nonviolence. The final volume discusses the dynamics of nonviolence, noting that in addition to conversion, both accommodation and nonviolent coercion are possible outcomes of a nonviolent campaign. To see how these can arise, it is necessarily to consider briefly Sharp's conception of power and resistance.

We might sum up Sharp's view of the source of nonviolent resistance in two claims. First, "that governments depend on people, that power is pluralistic, and that political power is fragile because it depends on many groups for reinforcement of its power sources."[22] Second, and closely related, "the sources of a ruler's power...depend *intimately* upon the obedience and cooperation of subjects."[23] Power depends on people, who in turn will give that power only through their obedience and cooperation. What this implies is that when people withdraw their cooperation, when they no longer obey, the power over them is lost. This view of power rests in the idea that it comes from below rather than above. Power is not something that is possessed by those who are often said to be "in power." Rather, it is granted to them by those over whom they are said to "have power."

To be sure, this does not mean that there is nothing to the idea that rulers and others in position of authority do not have any means at their disposal to exact cooperation. They do. They have access to police, to jails, to media, to surveillance, to material resources, and sometimes to extrajudicial sources, for example Mubarak's paid thugs who attempted to disrupt the occupation of Tahrir Square. Sharp does not deny the reality of any of these. Rather, what he points out is that they are only effective to the extent to which they can actually obtain obedience, and that that is dependent on the will of the people from which one seeks that obedience. As he puts the point, "*It is not the sanctions themselves which produce obedience but the fear of them.*"[24]

This idea might seem to be a bit counterintuitive. After all, one might say, isn't it reasonable to be afraid of beatings or jail or, in the extreme, death? Isn't there a deep bond between the resources to which a ruler has access and the obedience that people offer that ruler, such that it would seem forced or counterintuitive to say that power actually comes from below? Doesn't the ability of a ruler or others in position of political authority to utilize their resources really amount to their having power over people?

Sharp's claim, however, is not that it is always easy to withdraw obedience. As many people have emphasized, a strictly nonviolent campaign – particularly in the face of a callous adversary – requires discipline and often training. And we have seen that both Gandhi and King require prayer before entering into a more conflictual stage in a nonviolent campaign. The role of prayer is not simply to request the assistance of a deity, but more importantly to prepare oneself for the danger that may lie ahead. Gandhi prepared a set of rules for individuals to follow who are members of a nonviolent resistance campaign. Later, in the Birmingham, Alabama campaign, where protestors met with the extreme violence of Sheriff Bull Connor, volunteers were required to sign a Commitment Card, in which they pledged, among other things, to "Sacrifice personal wishes in order that all men might be free" and "Refrain from the violence of fist, tongue, and heart."[25] To say that power requires the cooperation of those over whom it is said to be exercised does not commit Sharp to the view that it is not difficult to refuse obedience, only to the view that without such obedience the power of the ruler collapses.

For Sharp, then, the dynamic of nonviolent resistance is wider than just the Gandhian one. For Gandhi, there is a moral jiu-jitsu whose result, when successful, is the conversion of the adversary. By contrast, Sharp does not require such conversion. He allows three possible results of a successful nonviolent campaign: conversion, accommodation, and coercion. Regarding the latter two, "In *accommodation* the opponent chooses to grant demands and to adjust to the new situation which has been produced without changing his viewpoint. Where *nonviolent coercion* operates, change is achieved against the opponent's will and without his agreement, the sources of his power having been so undercut by nonviolent means that he no longer has control."[26] Sharp uses the term *political* jiu-jitsu rather than *moral* jiu-jitsu to refer to the process of nonviolent change. This distinction marks the important difference between political change and moral conversion. Moral conversion may be one way in which political change takes place, but nonviolence does not require it. The Gandhian dynamic is one among several dynamics that may take place in a successful nonviolent campaign.

One of those who have studied the dynamics of nonviolence in specific conditions is Kurt Schock, whose book *Unarmed Insurrections* focuses on nonviolent resistance campaigns in nondemocracies, especially in South Africa, the Philippines, Burma, China, Nepal, and Thailand. He argues, contrary to the necessity of a Gandhian approach, "Nonviolent action does not depend on moral authority, the 'mobilization of shame' or the conversion of the views of the opponent in order to promote political change. While conversion of the opponent's views sometimes occurs, more often than not nonviolent action promotes political change through nonviolent coercion, that is, it forces the opponent to make changes by undermining the opponent's power."[27] Schock's position is in keeping with Sharp's that power requires obedience, and like Sharp he does not require moral conversion in order for there to be nonviolent political change.

This leaves us with several questions. First, what might political jiu-jitsu look like without moral conversion? Can there be the former without the latter, and will it still be something that can reasonably be called nonviolent? Second, are there dynamics of nonviolence that don't take the form of political jiu-jitsu? And, as with the former, can they reasonably be called nonviolent? Sharp himself admits of the latter possibility, noting that "Political *jiu-jitsu* does not operate in all nonviolent struggles... If opponents become more sophisticated in dealing with nonviolent action, so that they drastically reduce, or even eliminate violent repression and thereby political jiu-jitsu, the nonviolent actionists will still be able to win."[28] The questions are: by what dynamics might they be able to do so, and will those dynamics still preserve the dignity of the adversary by not subjecting them to physical, psychological, or structural violence?

Before turning to nonviolence without political jiu-jitsu, however, we should consider the first possibility of political jiu-jitsu without moral conversion. If we recall the Philippine anti-Marcos campaign, we can see an example of it. In fact, we can see both moral conversion and nonviolent coercion in play at the same time. The political jiu-jitsu stems primarily, although not solely, from the events that followed the 1983 murder of Benigno Aquino, an act whose effects rebounded in the form of a decreasing political legitimation of the Marcos regime and a destabilization of the business environment. Those in turn led to increased legitimization of the opposition and the alignment of the business community with that opposition. The fraudulent conduct of the 1986 election continued this cycle of repression that breeds opposition, this time leading to rebellion not only in the civilian population but also in the military one. Each major act of oppression made it more difficult to maintain the fiction of the regime's moral authority, which in turn helped solidify the opposition within the three groups to which Sharp calls our attention: the uncommitted (ex. businesses), the grievance group (the populace whose resolve grew with increased oppression), and eventually members of the adversary group itself (especially the military).

The moral conversion in the anti-Marcos campaign is of the troops sent to attack the rebel soldiers and who then refused to fire on the civilians surrounding the headquarters of the defense ministry. There is no reason to believe, however, that Ferdinand Marcos was ever converted to the beliefs of those who rebelled against his rule. In his case, there was coercion pure and simple. Now it might be argued that this coercion was not due solely to the internal protests from the rebel military and their civilian protectors. The end of support from the United States undoubtedly played a role in convincing Marcos that his time as President of the Philippines was over. While this is true, the withdrawal of US support is itself due to the unwillingness of the Filipino people to be governed any longer by Marcos. In Sharp's terms, their obedience had been withdrawn, and with it the ability of the USA to excuse underwriting his regime in the name of anti-communism.

Was Marcos' coerced exit from the Philippines nonviolent? There is every reason to believe so. He certainly was not assaulted physically or abused psychologically, and the circumstances of his leaving were comfortable enough that it would be a stretch to say that he was subject to anything analogous to structural violence. If we turn to the more rigorous definition of the type of violence that nonviolence seeks to avoid – disrespect for the dignity of others – we also fail to find grounds for saying the forced exit was violent. To be sure, Marcos was no longer able to continue to lead the life he had led, one which required oppression and violence against others in order to be sustained. However, he was still able to live a decently human life, to have his basic needs met, and to be protected from various forms of abuse that might have come to him from the desire for revenge among many of his erstwhile subject Filipinos. In this way, and contrary to practices of imprisoning or executing former dictators, his treatment after abandoning the Presidency cannot even arguably be classified as violent. (Whether imprisoning former dictators amounts to nonviolence or instead to justified violence is a question we can leave to the side.)

Much the same dynamic can be seen in the events at Tahrir Square, where increasing oppression leads to decreased legitimacy and eventually to the coerced exit of a dictator. However, the dynamic of political jiu-jitsu need not only be seen in regard to a dictatorial regime. The US Civil Rights movement at times consciously evoked the working of political jiu-jitsu in its attempt to garner the support of the American people. This can be seen particularly in the case of the Birmingham campaign.[29] That campaign was launched in the wake of the failure of the campaign in Albany, Georgia. There the sheriff Laurie Pritchett had stymied the movement to integrate bus and railroad lines as well as lunch counters by refusing to act violently against the protestors. Instead, he instructed his officers to arrest protestors without incident and he contacted surrounding jails so that there would be enough room to accommodate arrests. This tactic turned out to be exemplary of a situation in which, as Sharp claims, "opponents become more sophisticated in dealing with nonviolent action, so that they drastically reduce, or even eliminate violent repression and thereby political jiu-jitsu." The Albany movement eventually ran out of steam, which resulted in a critical moment for the Civil Rights movement.

Fortunately for them, not all Southern sheriffs possessed the sophistication of a Laurie Prichett. As the Reverend Fred Shuttlesworth argued to King and others, Birmingham's Sheriff Eugene "Bull" Connor would be happy to provide the kinds of images that would garner sympathy among those who needed education about conditions of blacks in the South, i.e. would provide the repressive element necessary for political jiu-jitsu. Connor did, but only after a sustained campaign whose most controversial tactic turned out to be its most effective one. Birmingham had been the object of protests before it became the focus of the 1963 campaign, but the arrival of King and his associates made it the temporary center of the Civil Rights campaign. Protestors held sit-ins at various segregated locations, "kneel-ins" in front of segregated white churches, and voter registration campaigns. They were arrested and brought to the Birmingham jail. Difficulties for the movement developed, however, when it seemed there were not enough people willing to risk jail in order to protest. This was understandable, since those jailed would not be able to provide for their families, many of whom were already living in an economically tenuous situation.

During the course of the protests, King decided to make himself available for arrest. While in jail, he penned a letter on scraps of paper that challenged the "moderates," particularly among the clergy, to throw their weight behind the justice of the protests and demonstrations. "We know through painful experience," he wrote, "that freedom is never voluntarily given by the oppressor; it must be demanded by the oppressed...For years now I have heard the word 'Wait!' It rings in the ear of every Negro with piercing familiarity. This 'Wait' has almost always meant 'Never.' We must come to see, with one of our distinguished jurists, that 'justice too long delayed is justice denied.'"[30]

However, even King's arrest did not mobilize the black residents of Birmingham in the way that was hoped. The jails were not full, and white Birmingham was not feeling moral pressure. Then one of the campaign organizers, James Bevel, decided to mobilize a group that would not risk economic disaster for families, would already be in solidarity with one another, and would likely respond enthusiastically to the idea of going to jail as a form of rebellion: high school and even grade school students. Although attempts were made to block the students from protesting, on May 2 thousands of them gathered at the Sixteenth Street Baptist Church and spread across the city. In the days that followed, what became known as the "Children's Crusade," vilified by many both inside and outside the Civil Rights movement, quickly filled the jails and placed Birmingham on the defensive. Bull Connor's reaction was precisely what the Birmingham campaign's organizers had hoped for. When the jails could no longer hold any more students, he turned fire hoses and police dogs on the protestors. These tactics were caught on camera, presenting to the nation some of the most iconic images of the Civil Rights movement. It was these images, and the recognition that they crystallized the South's treatment of blacks, that led to the political jiu-jitsu that forced Birmingham officials to begin to come to terms with their segregationist history. In this case, the events following the campaign, especially the slowness of integration, show that what happened there was more a matter of accommodation mixed with coercion than conversion. The Birmingham campaign demonstrates that political jiu-jitsu is not confined to resistance against dictators like Marcos or Mubarak or foreign occupations as in the case of India, but is also effective against local structures of injustice, what were referred to in the previous chapter as instances of structural violence.

Although the two most famous nonviolent campaigns of the twentieth century – Gandhi's Indian Independence movement and the American Civil Rights movement – worked centrally, if not exclusively, through political jiu-jitsu, and although it seemed to Gandhi as though such jiu-jitsu is a necessary condition of nonviolence, to later students of nonviolence there has emerged a view that there can be nonviolent campaigns, and indeed successful ones, without it. There is something about political jiu-jitsu that is both romantic and morally compelling. It is romantic in the belief that expressions of human dignity in the face of repression can lead to changes through an appeal to people's consciences. In contrast to violent coercion, the character of a campaign that instead works through what we might loosely call "spiritual" methods claims our sympathy in a way that seems to elevate our humanity. It is morally compelling in that it seems to engage in this elevation by way of a path that appeals to our moral convictions. It is not that people are not forced to accept or at least accommodate to what Gandhi calls Truth. Rather, it is that, if we might put it this way, it is Truth rather than Power that they are forced to accept. Moreover, that forcing happens through a set of means that displays rather than degrades human dignity. (This dignity is distinct from – although related to – the dignity that is respected through nonviolence. It is instead a dignity that is *expressed* through nonviolence, and it will be discussed in the following chapter.)

If there are dynamics of nonviolence that do not work through moral or political jiu-jitsu, they must still operate, even when coercively, through a respect for the dignity of the adversary. Kurt Schock's *Unarmed Insurrections* is a study that focuses on resistance in nondemocracies, and his analysis points the way toward how such dynamics may be conceived. Before turning directly to his view, however, it is worth noting that one of the reasons he undertakes to study nonviolence in nondemocracies is to challenge the view that, as he puts it, "nonviolent action can succeed only in democracies and only when it is used against 'benign' or 'universalist' oppressors."[31] This view is founded on the idea that if an adversary is not benign or its violence is not contained, it will simply crush the nonviolent opponent. As we have already seen with the fall of Mubarak and of Marcos (one of Schock's case studies), even brutal dictators can be brought down through nonviolent action. Schock asks how this is possible.

He notes that in order for nonviolence to have a chance of success, there are two necessary conditions. "Two basic conditions must be met for a challenge to contribute to political transformations: (1) the challenge must be able to withstand repression, and (2) the challenge must undermine state power."[32] We have seen aspects of both of these conditions. Gene Sharp addresses the second condition in his insistence that obedience is the source of a ruler's power and that when that is withdrawn, the ruler no longer rules. The first condition is an element of moral or political jiu-jitsu. But it is only an element of it. Schock does not argue that the rebound effect of such a jiu-jitsu must take place in order for nonviolent action to succeed in nondemocracies, only that the movement be able to sustain itself during the inevitable repression that will result from a challenge to state power. How, then, do nonviolent movements do that?

The answer Schock gives is that withstanding repression comes from the internal resilience of the movement and the leverage they achieve. Resilience relies on several aspects of the movement. "Characteristics of unarmed struggles that enhance their resilience in the face of repression include decentralized yet coordinated organizational networks, the ability to implement multiple actions from across the three methods of nonviolent action [Sharp's protest and persuasion, noncooperation, and intervention], the ability to implement methods of dispersion as well as concentration, and tactical innovation."[33] In short, organizational and tactical flexibility are key elements of the resilience of a nonviolent movement. It is not difficult to see why. Where there is only a single tactic, say street protests or boycotts, it is easier for the adversary to focus its forces on that tactic in order to crush it. In addition, as we will see when we turn to the broader question of why nonviolence is successful, a multitude of tactics allow many individuals to participate, thus broadening the base of the movement. Similarly, where there is a centralized or hierarchical leadership, a nondemocratic state will find it easier to eliminate than a mobile one. However, as Schock notes, mobility does not imply chaos. Although flexible, nonviolent movements must also be capable of coordination. Otherwise they run the risk of working at cross-purposes and of being split through an adversary's strategy of divide and conquer.

Resilience alone is not enough, unless it can eventually undermine the control of the authority. In other words, in order to succeed resilience needs leverage. "*Leverage* refers to the ability of contentious actors to mobilize the withdrawal of support from opponents or invoke pressure against them through the networks upon which opponents depend for their power."[34] We can recall here the example of the conversion of the Filipino army units sent to attack the defense headquarters in the final confrontation with the Marcos regime, or, from the previous chapter, the economic pressure placed upon the Montgomery Bus Line through the loss of black ridership and the political pressure placed upon the city during the Montgomery Bus Boycott. Not all sites in a power structure are equally necessary for it to retain its hegemony. For nondemocracies in particular, the army is a crucial arena of sustenance. At times, so is control of the media or the nominally independent branches of government. When the support among these is eroded, leverage for transformation is created.

To illustrate the roles of leverage and resistance, Schock offers a quick contrast between the Solidarity movement in Poland during the 1980s and the Chinese occupation of Tiananmen Square in 1989. The former, founded in the formation of the first noncommunist trade union in communist Poland, spent nearly a decade opposing the communist regime, and in 1989 (the same year as the Tiananmen Square Massacre) forced authorities into partially free elections, which resulted in the leader of Solidarity, Lech Walesa, assuming the Presidency in 1990. The occupation of Tiananmen Square, by contrast, was crushed by an army intervention that killed hundreds of protestors. Although both movements were oppositional to nondemocratic regimes, there were in Schock's view five important differences between them that helped Solidarity succeed where Tiananmen failed.

First, the Polish movement unfolded over nearly a decade, and its roots were earlier than that, so that it was "gradually forging an oppositional civil society through boycotts and methods of creative nonviolent intervention."[35] Second, while the activities of Solidarity and its related organizations were coordinated, they were also dispersed. The protest in Tiananmen, by contrast, was concentrated into a single area. Third, because Solidarity was rooted in the workers at the shipyards and extended to other working people in Poland, the movement developed economic leverage lacked by the protestors at Tiananmen. Fourth, their goals were initially limited to recognition of the union itself and easing of state censorship, while the demands of the protestors in China were more diffuse. (Whether this is a necessary condition of the success of a nonviolent movement in general – as opposed to an insurrection against a nondemocratic state – is a question to which we will return at the end of the chapter.) Finally, Solidarity exhibited a resilience through its dispersion, its various forms of protest, and its willingness to buy time and wait for propitious moments. The protestors at Tiananmen, on the other hand, were limited in their time and their tactics by the limits of the occupation itself.

One might ask here why the occupation of Tahrir Square was effective where that of Tiananmen failed. There were, however, important differences. First, the protests in Egypt did not take place solely in Tahrir Square. They were spread across the country. Although the description in the first chapter focused on the Square, this was not the only place demonstrations were taking place. In addition, the protestors there – as opposed to those in China – gained important leverage when the Egyptian army refused to disperse them. This allowed them to continue to occupy the Square, buying them time that was not afforded to the Tiananmen protestors. To be sure, the time they needed was far less than that of the Solidarity movement. But the time necessary for successful resistance is relative to the specific struggle itself. In the Egyptian case, because of the specific circumstances under which it took place, a couple of weeks were all that was required for it to force Mubarak from office.

The analysis Schock gives does not require moral or political jiu-jitsu in order for nonviolence to be effective against nondemocratic regimes. The case of Solidarity may be one where jiu-jitsu did not play a central role. The anti-occupation resistance of the Estonians was another. It exemplifies well the characteristics of resistance to a nondemocracy that Schock isolates, one to a foreign occupation rather than an indigenous dictator – as was the Solidarity movement. (In the end, however, they were both struggles against the same foreign occupier, the Soviet Union, since that was the force behind the Polish dictatorship.) In the case of Estonia, there were both resilience and, eventually, leverage. The resilience came in the form, as Shock would have it, of "decentralized yet coordinated networks." There were the independence parties, the Estonian Heritage Society, the scientists and students in the "phosphate war," and of course the singing.

The leverage arose as a combination of the internal struggle and external fortune that came in the form of the weakening of the Soviet Union. At first, Russia found it more difficult to keep its far-flung empire in line. And later, it was no longer able to keep itself intact as a communist state. Without the latter, Estonia may still have gained its independence, although it would likely have taken longer. Without the former, it is not clear how much leverage the Estonians would have had. However, through a combination of resistance and internal Soviet decay, there was enough leverage to allow the nonviolent struggle of the Estonian people to survive long enough to see their independence.

This happened without the emergence of a form of political jiu-jitsu. The Soviet occupiers were not moved by the Singing Revolution, and the people of Estonia did not need to see acts of courage in order to be motivated to liberate themselves. To be sure, some of the early public demonstrations by courageous individuals must have motivated others to join the struggle. But the desire had long been there, to which the spontaneous outbreaks of singing "Land of My Fathers, Land that I Love" testify. What occurred in Estonia was a form of coercion that was a result of the combination of the withdrawal of obedience with the weakening of Soviet power, a combination that worked through the resilience of the movement and the opening of leverage, but without political jiu-jitsu.

We can also see nonviolent resistance working without political jiu-jitsu in another historical example, one that involves resistance to but not insurrection against an occupying power. This was the Danish resistance to the German occupation during World War II, and in particular its saving of almost the entirety of its Jewish population. When the Nazis invaded Denmark in 1940, the Danes offered little resistance, as indeed they had little resistance to offer. However, as it became clear that the German occupation was intended not simply to keep them neutral but instead to turn them into accomplices of the Nazi regime, popular unrest emerged in a variety of quarters.[36] There appeared underground publications, strikes, and occasionally acts of sabotage. However, the most enduring form of resistance was Denmark's successful campaign to save nearly all of its nearly 8000 Jews. In the fall of 1943, Germany High Command ordered the roundup of Jews. The plan was to surprise them in their homes while they were celebrating Rosh Hashanah, which would make the roundup easy. However, word was leaked to several Danes, who in turn leaked word to other Danes, both inside and outside the Jewish community.

Immediately attempts were made by Danes across the country to save the Jewish population. As historians Ackerman and DuVall recount, "Ambulance driver Jorgen Knudsen searched through local phone books for the addresses of families with 'Jewish-sounding names.' He then drove his ambulance to go warn them and, if they had nowhere to hide, took them either to the hospital or to homes of doctors active in the resistance. Other Jews were approached on the streets by total strangers who offered them keys to their apartments or houses."[37] Frustrated in their actions, the Germans turned up the heat on the Danish population, ordering them to turn over Danish Jews to the occupying authority. The Danish resistance responded by organizing clandestine boat lifts to ferry their Jews across the Kattegat Strait to Sweden, which was neutral in the war. (I have the good fortune to teach every summer in a house on the Danish shore from where I can see the embarkation point for many of those boat lifts. One looks across a peaceful stretch of water and sees Sweden lying across the way. At night the lights of Sweden blink across the Strait. One can only imagine the feelings of the Jews and their Danish supporters as they stood on the shore during those nights in the autumn of 1943.) In all, 7,220 Jews were safely spirited to Sweden, while only 427 were captured by the Nazis, and those during the Rosh Hashanah raids.[38] The Danish efforts on behalf of its Jewish population offer an example, alongside that of the Estonian resistance to the Soviet occupation, of nonviolence that does not work through the dynamic of moral or political jiu-jitsu. Although there was a backlash against the German authorities by the Danish population when the Nazis sought to capture Danish Jewry, that backlash did not provoke direct resistance to the occupation itself, which in this case would likely have proved futile. Rather, if anything, it reinforced Danish efforts to save their fellow Jews. Even this, however, was not central to the dynamic of Danish resistance in this area, since the Danes had already shown their willingness to protect the Jewish population during the first Nazi effort to round them up. And of course, since the boat lift involved only the frustration of the Nazi project of eliminating European Jewry, it meets the criterion for nonviolence articulated in the last chapter. It would certainly be awkward to argue that the boat lift violated in any way the dignity of the German occupiers.

Over the course of this chapter, we have seen several dynamics of nonviolent resistance. We first investigated the traditional Gandhian dynamic of resistance/repression/suffering/conversion. We then widened that focus to see forms of nonviolent accommodation and coercion. Both of these dynamics involve the deployment of moral or political jiu-jitsu, the rebounding back on the adversary of the consequences of their attempts to suppress nonviolent resistance. Finally, we investigated dynamics of nonviolence that do not require such jiu-jitsu as part of their structure. We have seen various examples of these, from part of the Indian Independence Movement in the early twentieth century to the more recent insurrection against former Egyptian President Hosni Mubarak. All of the struggles recounted briefly at the outset of this book have found their place in one or another of these dynamics, except one: New York Occupy.

Occupy seems either to promise a new form of nonviolent resistance or to mark a failed experiment in seeking to construct such a form. Its novelty does not stem from the fact of occupying a certain space and remaining there. As we have seen, the Egyptian resistance engaged in a public occupation.

There have been other occupations as well. In Brazil landless workers associated with the *Movimento dos Trabalhadores Sem Terra* or MST have occupied unused land owned by larger landowners in order both to work the land for their survival and to call attention to the disparaties in resource ownership in Brazil. In Argentina in the early 2000s, the "recovered factory movement" saw workers occupying and running factories that had been abandoned or from which they had been fired in the wake of the 2001 economic crisis. (We will return to these two movements in our final chapter.) What makes Occupy different from these is that it did not have a distinct set of demands, particularly at the outset. It was more of an announcement that the 99 percent are here. To be sure, it had a critical edge, but this edge never coalesced into a specific set of demands. It remained a criticism of what might be called neoliberalism (also discussed in the final chapter), and an invitation to others to act as they saw fit.

In this way, Occupy is closer to a movement like Critical Mass. Critical Mass is a "protest" movement of bicycling, which began in San Francisco in 1992, in which cyclists gather en masse to ride in city streets that are normally used by automobile traffic.[39] Their motto is "We are not blocking traffic. We are traffic." The goals of Critical Mass are a bit diverse, but fundamentally they want to reclaim roads for bicycling instead of more polluting forms of traffic and to highlight the often dangerous disrespect cyclists undergo in cities where cars are considered, in practice if not in theory, to have the right of way. Although Critical Mass does not retain the participation or energy it once did, at its height it involved tens of thousands of riders in hundreds of cities, and was successful in calling attention to the need for more protections for road cyclists.

Occupy shares three important elements with Critical Mass. First, it has been a decentered movement, arising spontaneously in dozens of cities just as Critical Mass did. Second, it is focused on the occupation of space. While Critical Mass sought to occupy the streets in a moving pattern, Occupy took up particular spaces in particular cities; nevertheless, the occupation of space has been central to both. Third, both engage in a particular form of direct action, one that works not primarily by demand but instead simply by "being there."

In order to understand this third element, something should be said about the concept of direct action, which is often characteristic of nonviolence.

Direct action can best be seen in contrast to what might be called indirect action, in which one asks someone else to act on one's own behalf. For instance, going to a representative of a congressional or parliamentary body and asking to have a law or policy enacted is a form of indirect action. One is not undertaking the action oneself, but instead lobbying someone else to have it done. By contrast, in direct action one undertakes the action oneself. When blacks and whites in the American Civil Rights Movement sat down together at lunch counters or boarded interstate buses together in the South, they did not ask anyone to desegregate those lunch counters or buses but did it themselves directly. Nonviolence is often categorized by forms of direct action: the occupation of Tahrir Square or the front of the Filipino defense ministry, the singing of "Land of My People, Land that I Love," walking on the Vykom Temple Road, engaging in an economic or political boycott in solidarity with an indigeneous movement. Although nonviolence is not necessarily a form of direct action – we saw in the previous chapter that writing a letter to a representative could be seen as a minimal form of nonviolence – much of what has gone under the banner of nonviolent struggle has been in the form of direct action.

What characterizes Occupy and Critical Mass as nonviolent struggles is that it is less in what they are asking and more in the action itself, the "being there," that the struggle takes place. Occupy began without any demands at all, and when demands were drawn up they were diffuse and oriented less toward meeting specific goals than toward calling attention to current conditions. Critical Mass, one could say, accomplishes its goals simply by happening. If one gathers enough cyclists onto a road and rides alongside them, the streets then become reclaimed. This quality of "being there" is indicated in the role of the word *are* in the slogans of the two movements: We *are* the 99%, We *are* traffic. This characteristic of protest as "being there by way of occupation" contrasts sharply with many traditional nonviolent movements, which often sought concrete goals such as the desegregation of lunch counters or the Vykom Temple Road or the end of external occupation or internal dictatorship. We will return in the final chapter to the question of the role and prospects for nonviolence in the current world, but it should be noted here that Occupy and related movements offer a different model of nonviolence with a different dynamic from those we have discussed. Whether such movements are to be successful remains to be seen.

At the outset of this chapter we noted Chenoweth and Stephan's study of nonviolence, which showed that in anti-regime and anti-occupation struggles, nonviolence has been a far more effective form of struggle than nonviolence over the past century or more. They offer a number of reasons for this success, some of which we have already seen in discussion of the writings of Gandhi, Sharp, Schock, and others. However, to conclude this chapter it would be worth bringing these together, and Chenoweth and Stephan do an excellent job of detailing why nonviolence in its different dynamics tends to be more successful than violent movements. In the course of their study, eight factors emerge favoring nonviolent action: greater avenues for participation, the production of divisions within the adversary, backfiring (moral or political jiu-jitsu), the promise of safe exit for an adversary, the promotion of tactical diversity, greater resilience, the greater likelihood of receiving international or diplomatic support, and the consequence that nonviolence is more likely to lead to a democratic future. Although their study is confined to anti-occupation, anti-regime, and secessionist movements, their results are more widely applicable.

For Chenoweth and Stephan, the existence of greater avenues of participation is crucial to building a resistance movement, and one of the key reasons nonviolent movements have greater success than violent ones. This is a lesson that was not lost on either King or Gandhi. With regard to the Birmingham movement, King wrote, "In a nonviolent army, there is room for everyone who wants to join up. There is no color distinction. There is no examination, no pledge, except that, as a soldier in the armies of violence is expected to inspect his carbine and keep it clean, nonviolent soldiers are called upon to examine and burnish their greatest weapons – their heart, their conscience, their courage and their sense of justice."[40] For his part, Gandhi wrote specifically that noncooperation "is even open to children of understanding and can be practiced by the masses."[41] Gandhi did, however, distinguish noncooperation from civil disobedience, which to his mind required greater training and discipline.

The existence of these lower barriers to participation in nonviolence is largely due to the fifth and sixth factors Chenoweth and Stephan discuss: tactical diversity and a consequent resilience. Demonstrations, civil disobedience, letter-writing, information dissemination through leaflets or other media outlets, sit-ins, strikes, boycotts, etc. are all parts of many successful nonviolent campaigns. Where one is attacked, others can arise, and the existence of these different ways of participating allows people to enter into the struggle in whatever ways they feel comfortable and according to their own personal strengths.

One stark example of the importance of these lower barriers lies in the difference between the first Palestinian intifada of 1987–93 and the second one that ran from 2000–5. Both were directed against the Israeli occupation of Palestinian land. However, the first one relied importantly on nonviolence while the second one was almost solely violent. Although the first intifada involved rock-throwing at Israeli soldiers, it was mostly conducted through nonviolent demonstration, information dissemination, the production of an alternative economy to support participants during the many Israeli curfews that were imposed on the population, refusal to pay taxes, and strikes and closures. It brought enormous attention and sympathy to the plight of the Palestinian people, and played a role in the ratification of the (eventually failed) Oslo Accords. By contrast, the second intifada was conducted largely through the violence of the Palestinian police and security forces as well as suicide bombers, and gained the Palestinians nothing, even in the short term.

Before proceeding, it is worth pausing over the tactic of boycotts, a common one in nonviolent struggle. Sharp devotes a number of pages to a discussion of economic boycotts as among the methods of nonviolent struggle.[42] However, it is not clear to me that boycotts always fall on the nonviolent side of struggle. I believe that they can be either violent or nonviolent, depending on the context. In particular, external boycotts – boycotts coming from outside the context – are more likely to be nonviolent when there is an indigenous campaign with which the boycott is in solidarity, and less likely to be so in the absence of such a campaign. The sanctions placed on South Africa near the end of apartheid, in addition to being effective, were, I would argue, nonviolent, while those placed against Iraq after the first Persian Gulf War were violent. This is because in the former case the dignity of neither the black South African people nor the whites was violated, while in the latter the dignity of the Iraqi people was severely violated.

In South Africa, the privileged whites, while feeling pressure to change, were not undermined in their ability to lead a fully human life, that is, as mentioned earlier, *to engage in projects and relationships that unfold over time; to be aware of one's death in a way that affects how one sees the arc of one's life; to have biological needs like food, shelter, and sleep; to have basic psychological needs like care and a sense of attachment to one's surroundings.* And black South Africans did not have their dignity violated by the sanctions for two reasons. First, they shared little in the riches of the country, so economic losses would harm them less significantly than it would harm white South Africans. Second, and more important, the sanctions were in support of an existing struggle of black South Africans, and so rather than denying them their dignity sanctions were directly in support of it. The anti-apartheid movement within South Africa *asked* for sanctions. Therefore, the boycott of South Africa under apartheid contributed to the struggle and, partly because of this, was nonviolent.

By contrast, the sanctions that were orchestrated by the USA in the United Nations against Iraq after the first Persian Gulf War, from 1990–2003, while doing nothing to undermine its rule or even weaken it, did plenty of damage to the civilian population. Hundreds of thousands of people are estimated to have died from malnutrition, lack of potable water, the absence of medical supplies, and other necessary resources for sustaining the health of the population.[43] These sanctions did not intersect with any resistance movement – since there was no resistance movement to speak of – and were therefore not endorsed by those who bore the brunt of the suffering. They were thus neither voluntarily undergone in the attempt to struggle for a decent life nor a contributant to such a life: in fact, quite the opposite. Given the contrast, then, between different kinds of boycotts, the question of whether a boycott is or is not nonviolent can only be answered by looking at the context in which it takes place.

Returning to Chenoweth and Stephan's analysis, the second and third factors – divisions within the adversary and moral or political jiu-jitsu – we have already seen at length. The latter factor is almost entirely unavailable to violent resistance, since such resistance seems to place both resister and adversary on the same moral plane, at least as far as tactical engagement goes. This can be seen clearly in campaigns where technologically primitive terrorism is condemned just as strongly as more technologically advanced weaponry used by an adversary, as in the second Palestinian intifada or the early communist insurrection against Ferdinand Marcos in the Philippines. Moreover, moral or political jiu-jitsu can be a factor in garnering the seventh factor, diplomatic support. (Chenoweth and Stephan note that external *material* support is often greater for violent insurrections. Of course, much of that material support is irrelevant to nonviolent struggles.) It is difficult for international or external bodies to stand by when a nonviolent struggle is being ruthlessly suppressed.

And although both violent and nonviolent campaigns can cause divisions in the adversary, there are more avenues for such divisions to open up in nonviolent campaigns. In addition to the effectiveness of moral or political jiu-jitsu that we have seen in various campaigns, there is also the fourth factor, the promise of safe exit for an adversary. If an adversary or one of its members believes that he or she will be killed by a violent insurrection, that gives a motivation to keep struggling rather than surrender. However, if one knows that one's life is not at risk through surrender or exile, that option becomes more tempting. The more tempting it is for some among the adversary, the more likely divisions will arise within it.

The final factor, the greater likelihood of a democratic political order arising from a nonviolent campaign, is both intuitively plausible and empirically supported. As the twentieth century has shown through the contrast of violent insurrections like the Russian and Chinese revolutions with nonviolent ones, such as the Indian Independence movement, democracies rarely arise from the barrel of a gun. Those who have gained power through violence have a built-in hierarchical order in the resistance that does not have a counterpart in nonviolence, an issue to which we will return in the fifth chapter. If, as is sometimes said, power corrupts and absolute power corrupts absolutely, the distinction between those who possess and those who don't possess guns will tilt the former toward a more absolute form of power – unless, of course, there is a concerted nonviolent campaign against them, the would-be liberators.

Chenoweth and Stephan offer empirical backing for this view. As they conclude from their study, "Successful nonviolent campaigns increase the probability of democratic regime type by over 50 percent compared with successful violent insurgencies. Holding other variables constant, the probability that a country will be a democracy five years after a campaign ends is 57 percent among successful nonviolent campaigns but less than 6 percent for successful violent campaigns."[44] Moreover, "Countries in which a violent campaign has occurred have a 42 percent chance of experiencing a recurrence of civil war within ten years, compared with 28 percent for countries in which a nonviolent campaign has occurred."[45]

This chapter has investigated various dynamics of nonviolent resistance, from Gandhi's dynamic that requires conversion to other dynamics that allow for accommodation and even coercion, and from dynamics that operate on the basis of moral or political jiu-jitsu to dynamics that don't. We have also investigated the ways in which these dynamics are nonviolent in the sense discussed in the previous chapter. In the course of all this, we have also moved from the more philosophical reflections of the character of nonviolence to a variety of examples and studies of nonviolent campaigns. The following two chapters will bring us back to more philosophical investigations of nonviolence, but without losing the thread of the examples from this chapter (and adding a few others). Specifically, we will turn toward a more sustained investigation of two values that underlie nonviolence: dignity and equality. The first was discussed in the previous chapter; however, there is more to say about the character of dignity and its role in nonviolent struggle and resistance. Equality, by contrast, has been implicit throughout but needs to be made more explicit if we are to understand its role in nonviolence. In contrast to violence, dignity and equality are central values embraced by nonviolence, which in addition to their strategic role in contributing to successful campaigns, also lends nonviolence a normative power that can elevate the humanity of a struggle even in the most difficult and vulnerable of political situations.

4

The Values of Nonviolence: Dignity

Nonviolence expresses two central values, that of dignity and of equality. That is to say, nonviolent activity treats others in such a way as to respect their dignity and presuppose their equality. The dignity and the equality of others is important and to be respected. These seem like straightforward claims. After all, we have already offered a definition of dignity, and what could equality mean in nonviolence other than that the dignity of the other is equal to my own? However, as we will see over the next two chapters, there is more to these concepts than what has been presented so far. Regarding dignity, while it is true that we have given a definition of it as what is to be respected in nonviolence, investigating the concept further will allow us to deepen our understanding not only of how one treats the other but how the nonviolent actor relates to himself or herself. And regarding equality, we still need to ask what it is, how it relates to dignity, and what role it plays in nonviolent activity.

In philosophy, dignity and equality are sometimes seen as belonging to two different types of philosophical investigation. Dignity belongs to ethics or morality, while equality is a matter of political philosophy. Seen this way, dignity is a matter of how individuals treat – or better, *ought* to treat – one another in their individual relationships. Equality, on the other hand, has to do with the structure of social or political groups. It is not concerned with how each individual relates to each other individual, but rather with each individual's place in the larger social order. For example, if equal opportunity is a political value, this means that every individual in the society ought to have the same opportunity as others to obtain the social goods on offer. It does not mean that each individual has to offer every other individual some sort of equal opportunity to obtain those goods.

In nonviolence, the distinction between the ethical or the moral and the political or the social is not nearly as relevant as it is in traditional philosophy. The reason for this is not far to seek. Nonviolence seeks to be an ethical form of political action. It strives to act politically in a way that sees its adversary in ethical terms. In nonviolence, the ethical and the political are woven together. As a result, dignity will have political as well as ethical ramifications, and equality will have ethical as well as political ones. As the next two chapters unfold, this will become manifest with regard to each concept. However, it is worth pausing for a moment about the way in which the ethical character of nonviolence challenges the traditional approach of political philosophy.

One way of characterizing the difference between traditional ethical and political thought, admittedly a bit primitively, would be to contrast the images of "bottom-up" and "top-down" approaches. Ethics or morality (for our purposes, there is no need to distinguish between the two) is bottom-up, while traditional political philosophy is top-down. A bottom-up approach would see a good or just society as one that is to be built from the individual relationships. It would be the result of each individual treating other individuals in an ethically proper way. To the extent that each individual is treating all the other individuals with, let's say dignity, a good society would result.

By contrast, top-down approaches start with social rules, and claim that to the extent that those rules are enacted and followed in a society, a good or just social arrangement will result. This is the approach of the dominant tradition in liberal political philosophy, that of contractarianism. Contractarianism, from the seventeenth-century philosopher Thomas Hobbes through the late twentieth-century philosopher John Rawls, argues that a just society would be the result of a proper set of social rules that would be reasonable for everyone to agree to follow, that is, a social contract. The philosophical problem is that of coming up with the proper rules to the contract. This approach starts, not with individual relationships, but with general rules themselves, asking which ones would be proper to enact in order to have a just society. It is top-down in this sense: it moves from a vision of the general rules for a proper society structure (for example, equal opportunity), and then asks how they should be applied to individuals, rather than asking how individuals should act with one another in order to form a good or just social order.

Nonviolence, as an ethical form of collective political action, is a type of activity that is at once political and bottom-up. It is political in that it seeks political change, whether changes in regimes, laws, or policies. It is bottom-up in that it involves movements by people banding together rather than by those who nominally hold political power. (I use the term "nominally" here in recognition of Sharp's insight that the power of those in authority is largely founded on the obedience of those over whom that power is to be exercised.) In contrast to contractarian political theory, it does not operate from a formal set of principles that constitute a blueprint for society, but rather from a vision (or set of related visions – since not all nonviolent movements have the same vision) of how people should be treated or treat one another. And in contrast to traditional political change, it generally does not operate through representatives that are appealed to in order to change laws or policies. As Schock notes, "Nonviolent action is noninstitutional, that is, it operates outside the bounds of institutionalized political demands."[1] Although it is noninstitutional, nonviolence is also in contrast to most noninstitutional violent political change (terrorism would be an exception here) in that the latter often seeks top-down change by taking over the political levers in order to effect change rather than, as with nonviolence, undermining their ability to operate effectively.

This does not mean that every action in a nonviolent campaign must operate outside such channels. For instance, as we have seen, writing a letter to a Congressional representative in support of a nonviolent campaign can be an act that forms part of a nonviolent movement. Moreover, in accordance with the definition of nonviolence offered in the second chapter, an entire traditional campaign can occur through representatives and be nonviolent in the sense we defined it: *political, economic, or social activity that challenges or resists a current political, economic, or social arrangement while respecting the dignity of its participants, adversaries, and others.* However, what usually goes under the name of nonviolence is something else: a largely noninstitutional activity that challenges the something structural in the society or political arrangement that is currently in place. We might say that while traditional political activity is often not violent, what goes under the name of nonviolence is largely noninstitutional. And as such, it is bottom-up rather than being or appealing to a top-down structure in its efforts to promote change.

We should note in passing that while traditional political activity is often not violent, it may yet be violent if it seeks to violate the dignity of others. This would be especially true of traditional political activity that seeks to reinforce structural violence. For instance, the campaigns in the USA to force marriage laws to be restricted to people of two genders violates the dignity of those who are not heterosexuals. I would argue that overly restrictive laws against abortion violate the dignity of women. And in the USA, recent policy changes that eliminate food supplements to the poor and extended unemployment benefits (these are happening as I write these lines in early 2014) reinforce a structural violence against those who, often through no fault of their own, find themselves in difficulties over making ends meet. In thinking about nonviolence, then, we must not restrict our gaze to overt acts of violence. As I argued when defining nonviolence, the violence that nonviolence abjures is not only physical and psychological but also structural violence. That is the deeply ethical core of nonviolence, the core that makes it something that is not only a matter of policy or regime change but also an ethical vision of how people might relate to one another. And in nonviolence, this ethical core is not only *envisioned*, it is also *enacted*. As one of the current slogans has it, nonviolence counsels its participants to "be the change you want to see."

That change involves a respect for the dignity and equality of others. In order to investigate it more closely, let's first turn our attention to dignity and in the following chapter to equality, recognizing that both terms, while distinct, are related (in ways we shall see) and that in nonviolence they are both at once ethical and political values.

In the second chapter we referred briefly to Michael Rosen's book *Dignity*, which offers a brief history of the term. Dignity, as he recounts it, was originally a term of status. It designated the elevated place of some people in a hierarchy. However, with the Roman orator Cicero *dignitas* was transformed into a term that elevated humanity rather than just certain individuals within it. This idea was taken up within the Catholic tradition and then associated broadly with the idea of intrinsic value. This intrinsic value was not restricted to human beings, but attached in different ways to different beings depending on their place in God's cosmic order.

Intrinsic value, as opposed to instrumental value, is the value something has in and of itself. For example, money has almost solely instrumental value. Its value lies in its being able to purchase things. If we think of human beings as having not solely instrumental value but also intrinsic value, then we think that there is something about them that is valuable above and beyond their ability to advance our interests. For the Catholic tradition, then, different beings might have different types of intrinsic value, but all of them gained their value by virtue of their being products of the Creation.

The development of the term, however, is one that Rosen insists should not be seen simply as a linear progression from meaning to meaning. As he notes, in a text of Francis Bacon's from 1623 there are several meanings of *dignitate* at work. "We can see here three quite different meanings – dignity as valuable characteristic not restricted to human beings, dignity as high social status, and dignity as behavior with a certain respect-worthy character (or indignity as behavior lacking it) – coexisting in a single author in the early modern period, just as they seem to do today."[2]

It is with the philosopher Immanuel Kant that a significant development of the term takes place, one that sees dignity as a particularly human characteristic founded in humanity's being the sole possessor of rationality and therefore of the ability to act in accordance with morality. "While Aquinas' idea sees dignity of different kinds, potentially at least, at all levels of God's creation (perhaps even including plants), Kant's conception is restricted to human beings. Only human beings (so far as we know) are capable of acting morally and feeling the force of morality's claims."[3] We will return at length to Kant's discussion, but before that we should recall that, for Rosen, there are in the end four strands in the history of the term dignity. The first three strands are "the idea of dignity as status, the idea of dignity as inherent value, and the idea of dignity as behavior, character, or bearing that is dignified."[4] Kant's view would be a version of the second, restricted to human beings. But, he argues, "the third strand examined, the idea of dignity as behavior that is dignified, reveals a fourth: a perspective on dignity from which to treat someone *with dignity* is to treat them with respect. Instead of respecting dignity by respecting a set of fundamental rights, dignity requires respectfulness."[5]

For Rosen, the importance of this fourth strand of the concept of dignity is that it seems to reveal a kind of dignity that, rather than being the foundation of rights – as a term like intrinsic value might seem to imply – instead makes it a kind of particular right itself. However, for our purposes this fourth strand will operate differently, although not in opposition to Rosen's use of it. To anticipate, to act with dignity in nonviolent action (the third strand) involves treating someone with the proper respect (the fourth strand), tying together the dignity of the nonviolent actor with that of his or her adversary. This will require focusing on the second strand – intrinsic value. In order to see how this works, and to tie it together with the idea of dignity proposed in the second chapter and with examples of nonviolent action itself, it is worth pausing over Kant's view of dignity, that is, his version of the second strand. Although ultimately we will seek to move beyond it, it forms the philosophical foundation for much thinking about dignity, and the reflections here owe much to it.

For Kant, as Rosen notes, dignity is founded in morality. Morality, in turn, cannot be founded in the consequences of one's behavior, but must instead lie in one's intentions. That is to say, if we were to put it in a catch phrase, morality for Kant is not a matter of doing *good*, but instead of *doing* good. It is not the results of one's behavior that make an action moral, but instead what animates the behavior itself. As Kant says at the opening of his *Groundwork of the Metaphysic of Morals*, "It is impossible to conceive anything at all in the world, or even outside of it, which can be taken as good without qualification, except a *good will*."[6] But what makes a will a good one? What constitutes a good intention?

We often think of a good will or intention as arising out of sympathy or fellow feeling. But in Kant's view, this cannot be right. If it were, then morality would be subject to what we happened to have such feeling for. Some people might have a fellow feeling for people of their own race or gender, while others have sympathy for dogs more than for humans. There would be no consistency to morality if it were founded in feeling, just as if morality were founded in consequences it would be subject to luck. (Some actions cause better consequences through the good fortune of being in the right place at the right time rather than through foresight or even meaning to do good.) Morality must be founded in sturdier stuff than feeling or consequences. It must be founded in reason, and in pure reason at that.

Kant's argument about what constitutes pure reason – or in the case of morality what he calls pure practical reason – is subtle, but the broad idea is that whatever morality asks of us, it cannot be subject to anything empirical but must be a matter of reason divorced from empirical considerations. To put it in his terms, morality must involve imperatives that are categorical rather than hypothetical. A hypothetical imperative says, "If x, then do y." But that is a matter of doing y if you want x to happen. It makes the x itself subject to empirical considerations (what you want, what empirical results are worthwhile, etc.). By contrast, a categorical imperative says, "Do y." Morality, then, must be founded in a categorical imperative or imperatives that is itself (or themselves) founded in reason alone. This leads him to his famous formulations of the categorical imperative.

The first formulation of the categorical imperative, which will concern us less than two of the others, is "*Act only on that maxim through which you can at the same time will that it should become a universal law*."[7] Roughly, the idea is that you could will it that everyone in the relevantly same circumstances could act in just the way you propose to do. One classic example of something that cannot be so willed would be lying. If everyone lied, then nobody would believe anything that anybody said. And if nobody believed anyone else, then lying would lose its point. Lying only works against a background of truth-telling, where people believe one another. Therefore, lying cannot be something that one could will to be a universal law. And so one should not lie.

Kant offers three other formulations of the categorical imperative, all of which he thinks are equivalent to one another, that is, they will mutually imply one another. The second formulation is *"Act in such a way that you always treat humanity, whether in your own person or in the person of another, never simply as a means, but always as an end."*[8] The third formulation sets us up as both makers of and subject to the moral law: *"Act always on the maxim of such a will in us as can at the same time look upon itself as making a universal law."*[9] The final formulation is the one in which Kant's discussion of dignity appears. It is often called the "kingdom of ends" formulation. It can be seen as stemming most directly from the second formulation, where everyone, including oneself, is regarded as an end in itself rather than merely a means. Imagine yourself in a condition in which everyone treated everyone else as an end rather than merely a means. That would be a kingdom of ends, which, as Kant notes, "is admittedly only an Ideal."[10] To act in accordance with one's membership in a kingdom of ends would be to "act as if he were through his maxims always a law-making member in the universal kingdom of ends."[11]

It might seem at first glance that the idea of an end in itself and consequently that of a kingdom of ends is simply another way of formulating the concept of intrinsic value that we saw a moment ago in connection with the Catholic conception of dignity. However, for Kant, in accordance with the structure of his thought, only one thing can be treated as an end in itself, because there is only one thing that is "good without qualification," and that is a good will, which is to say pure practical reason. It is only such reason which is good, and therefore only such reason which is to be treated as an end in itself. The kingdom of ends, then, is a kingdom in which the pure practical reason of its members is both exercised by each and respected by the others.

This comes out especially in Kant's discussion of dignity. He says that, "In the kingdom of ends everything has either a *price* or a *dignity*. If it has a price, something else can be put in its place as an *equivalent*; if it is exalted above all price and so admits of no equivalent, then it has a dignity."[12] This sounds very much like the distinction between intrinsic and instrumental value. To have intrinsic value is to have some value in and of itself, not simply in reference to something else. It requires one to respect it for what it is, not simply use it for one's own ends. To have a dignity in Kant's sense is to be beyond price, to be unsubstitutable for anything else. And Kant himself confirms this equivalence when he writes, "that which constitutes the sole condition under which anything can be an end in itself has not merely a relative value – that is, a price – but has an intrinsic value – that is, *dignity*."[13] What is it, however, that has dignity? For Kant, the answer is clear: "morality, and humanity so far as it is capable of morality, is the only thing which has dignity."[14]

The first point to note here is that Kant does not say that only human beings have dignity. It is morality, not humans, that possesses dignity. That is to say, it is reason, or more precisely pure practical reason, that possesses dignity. Humans themselves possess dignity only inasmuch as they are capable of pure practical reason, that is, of following the categorical imperative. Kant confirms this idea when he writes in his summary of the categorical imperative, "we can now easily explain how it comes about that, although in the concept of duty we think of subjection to the law, yet we also at the same time attribute to the person who fulfills all his duties a certain sublimity and *dignity*. For it is not in so far as he is *subject* to the law that he has sublimity, but rather in so far as, in regard to this very same law, he is at the same time its *author* and is subordinated to it only on this ground."[15]

What is the picture of dignity Kant is placing before us? Recall that his discussion of dignity occurs within the context of his vision of morality as involving a kingdom of ends. This kingdom of ends is a kingdom of those who are capable of following the moral law, that is, the categorical imperative. But to be capable of following the moral law is not only to be subject to it in the way we are subject to traffic laws. One doesn't need to be capable of formulating the categorical imperative in order to do that. With a minimum of thought, I can recognize speed limits and red lights and learn how to follow them. In order to follow the moral law, one has to be capable of giving that law to oneself, of asking the question of what one should do, formulating a maxim that accords with the categorical imperative, and carrying it out. That is to say, one must at the same time be, in Kant's words, both author of and subject to the moral law. Moreover, in a kingdom of ends, one acts as though everyone were such authors and subjects – bearing in mind that such a kingdom is only an ideal. The dignity of human beings lies in their ability to do precisely that: act as though they (and we) were already members of a kingdom of ends.

At this point, we can begin to see parallels between Kant's vision of a kingdom of ends and nonviolent action. The parallels are loose, and in a moment I want to move slightly away from Kant's view, but there is already something in the way he envisions the kingdom of ends that speaks to nonviolence. In nonviolence, one does not treat the adversary as having a price, but rather as having an intrinsic value, a value that is to be respected. This treatment, as we saw in the second chapter, may be solely for pragmatic reasons rather than principled ones. However, as we also saw, the effect of that treatment is similar to a more principled nonviolence. In any event, the adversary is treated (if not regarded) as worthy of a certain respect. That is to say, he or she or it is treated as though they were not simply a means to one's own ends, but have a value that cannot be violated. And this is the case even where the adversary does not return the respect. One acts, as one is to act in Kant's view, *as though* one lived in a kingdom of ends, not *because* one lives in such a kingdom – of course, one does not. To put the point another way, in nonviolence one acts as a moral exemplar, not because one's adversary is doing so (if one is engaged in nonviolence one's adversary is probably not acting as a moral exemplar), nor even in order to get one's adversary to act that way (although the invitation to conversion is always there), but simply in order to be a moral exemplar. (Or, in the case of pragmatic nonviolence, one acts that way for the less Kantian reason that that is the best way to be at the moment for certain purposes.) The closer one is to more strictly Gandhian forms of nonviolence, the closer the parallels become.

And yet, the parallels between Kant's view and nonviolence are not those of strict identity. The reason for this has to do with Kant's conception of dignity. For him, dignity is a matter of the capacity to act in accordance with the moral law, the possession of pure practical reason. Recall that for him there is nothing absolutely good except a good will, that a good will consists in reason, and that it is the capacity for being able to act in accordance with such reason that constitutes the dignity of human beings. Is this the dignity that nonviolence respects? In the end, the answer is no, although it may seem so at first.

To see why it is something other than pure practical reason that is respected, let us consider one of our examples: the overthrow of Ferdinand Marcos. Of course, the campaign was directed not at his moral will but at his governance. Moreover, it was directed as well at the soldiers who were sent to support that governance. At the moment of confrontation, it was they as well as he who were the adversary. From a Kantian point of view, what would be respected in the nonviolent action would be the capacity of the soldiers to act in accordance with pure practical reason, that is, to be able to ask about their own actions whether they were in accord with the categorical imperative and to act out of the duty that implied in the situation. However, that seems too narrow a view of what was respected. Suppose a soldier had said to himself, "I don't want to be vilified for my actions, so I'd better not be the one firing on these protestors." That would not have been in accordance with the categorical imperative, and so would not count as a Kantian reaction. It is difficult to believe, however, that in respecting the dignity of the other a nonviolent campaign would count that as outside what is to be respected. Such a reaction would certainly count as an acceptable motive for refusing to act violently, and would be respected by nonviolent campaigners.

Would the Kantian view fare better with a more strictly Gandhian response on the part of the adversary? Suppose a soldier had said to himself, "These people are shaming me with the nobility of their willingness to suffer. When I ask myself whether attacking them is justified, I must answer no.

Moreover, their willingness to suffer is making me reconsider my support for the regime itself. After all, it is the regime that has sent me to harm my own people." The answer to the question of whether this conversion is Kantian or not would depend on the details of the soldier's moral considerations. If the soldier were acting out of a sense of duty that implies that anyone in his situation should do the same thing, then the response would be Kantian, and it can certainly be read that way. However, if the soldier were acting out of consequentialist reasons, thinking that the regime of Ferdinand Marcos is just worse for the Filipino people than another regime might be, and that therefore he shouldn't support Marcos, then his reasoning would not be Kantian. It would be, in the terms we discussed earlier, a hypothetical rather than a categorical imperative: "If Marcos goes, then it will be better for the Filipino people."

It would be difficult to imagine that a Gandhian would require a strictly Kantian set of reasons for conversion as the basis of the dignity of the other to be respected. The capacity for conversion does not require that one be converted for reasons in accordance with the categorical imperative, much less for reasons that arise solely out of what Kant sometimes calls respect for the moral law. Conversion casts a wider net. So, while it is possible that one could be converted for Kantian reasons, the respect for the dignity of the other implied by a Gandhian campaign seeking conversion need not imply such a narrow view of dignity.

Instead, that dignity must have a more expansive provenance, one closer to what is implied in our second chapter. It is not simply the ability to act in accordance with the categorical imperative that is respected by nonviolence, but more broadly the having of a human life to lead, that is, roughly, *the ability to engage in projects and relationships that unfold over time; to be aware of one's death in a way that affects how one sees the arc of one's life; to have biological needs like food, shelter, and sleep; to have basic psychological needs like care and a sense of attachment to one's surroundings.* This broader definition allows that people might respond to nonviolence in a variety of ways, of which a Kantian response is only one. They may respond with other types of conversion, such as the more consequentialist one just cited. Or they may respond in a more self-interested fashion, but one that still accords with the goals of the movement, as with the imagined soldier who did not want to be personally vilified for his actions. Or they may respond with a rejection of the demands of the movement, in which case more action is needed. But if that action is to be nonviolent, it must nevertheless, even when coercive, respect the human character of the adversary. It cannot force the adversary to do one's bidding at the cost of denying their dignity.

What would go for the soldiers in the Filipino case would hold just as strictly for Ferdinand Marcos himself. We are probably justified in assuming that Marcos was never converted to the protestors' cause. He was forced from office through the type of dynamic described by Sharp in which nonobedience leads to the collapse of authority. However, it was not demanded by the protests that he be killed or publicly paraded through the streets or even held in a jail cell for the rest of his life. He was allowed to live, albeit elsewhere, a life of human dignity. That dignity consisted not in the narrow sense of his ability to act according to the Kantian moral law. That was probably unknown to most of the protestors and irrelevant to others. Rather, the nonviolent protests, we might say, sought not to degrade him in his person. The wider definition of dignity offered in the second chapter captures this idea, although its affinities – particularly in structure – with Kant's own view are not to be denied.

We have, throughout this book, been concerned with the issue of particularly *human* dignity. The question might be raised of how to think about nonviolence in regard to nonhuman animals. The reason we have focused on human as opposed to nonhuman nonviolence is that the context here is nonviolent *resistance* – campaigns and movements that seek political change through nonviolent means. In this case, the adversaries in particular are going to be other humans, as will many of the bystanders. Even in cases where the resistance is to particularly egregious treatment of nonhuman animals, such as certain types of laboratory research or anti-whaling campaigns – those whose actions are being challenged are not the nonhuman animals themselves but the humans who are disregarding their interests. However, there may well be bystanders or other third parties that, in the course of a campaign of resistance, are at risk of violence of some sort and therefore require some respect. This respect cannot be exactly of the type described in the second chapter, because, among other things, most nonhuman animals do not have anything like projects and are not concerned in a long-term way with the fact of their deaths. So it might be asked what kind of dignity is to be respected by nonviolence in the case of nonhuman animals.

Such a consideration would bring us far from a Kantian ethics. It will be unsurprising for the reader to learn that for Kant, since nonhuman animals did not in his view possess the resources to act out of respect for the moral law, they had no dignity that need be respected. Any harm that was done to them could only be morally suspect as a violation of the rights of that animal's owner. This is likely not the consensus among many people today. However, in order to sort this issue out and offer an adequate account of the particular dignity one must accord to nonhuman animals, it would be necessary to engage the literature on animals rights, which is characterized not so much by any consensus on this matter but by its absence. That would carry us too far afield. We will need to be content to note that a nonviolent campaign must recognize that many nonhuman animals also have lives to lead – lives that allow them to flourish as the kind of animals they are – and that, as bystanders, the interests of those animals must be taken into account. As a rule of thumb, we could say that nonviolence should avoid the torture or killing of nonhuman animals, and seek to protect their interests inasmuch as the actions of a campaign have bearing on those interests. That is probably as far as we can go without offering a detailed account of the particular dignity of different species. Fortunately, since most nonviolent campaigns of the sort we are concerned with here only affect nonhuman animals marginally, this is probably as far as we need to go.[16]

Returning to the thread of discussion, we have been considering Kant's use of the term dignity, which is the second "strand" of dignity in Michael Rosen's discussion of its history. This is "the idea of dignity as behavior, character, or bearing that is dignified." As he notes, "the idea of dignity as behavior that is dignified, reveals a fourth: a perspective on dignity from which to treat someone *with dignity* is to treat them with respect." As we will see, the fourth strand is intimately bound to the third strand because the third strand is bound to the second one. But before we see this, we must see how the third strand operates in nonviolent action.

The importance of dignified behavior is recognized by Joan Bondurant in her discussion of suffering in Gandhi's conception of satyagraha. "The element of self-suffering," she writes, "in satyagraha is perhaps, of all three fundamentals [truth, ahimsa, self-suffering], the least acceptable to a Western mind. Yet, such sacrifice may well provide the ultimate means of realizing that characteristic so eminent in Western moral philosophy: the dignity of the individual."[17] How might this be? For Gandhi, the individual is the ultimate source of his or her own obedience or refusal. The dignity of the individual lies in one's ability to choose whether to assent to or resist the context in which one finds oneself, as for instance in the event which the cover of this book records. As his biography shows, Gandhi often displayed this lesson in his own life, and he believed that it was up to others not to sacrifice their own dignity for the sake of some type of convenience. This idea, of course, is tied to his notion of Truth, which nobody has completely but rather is the duty of each to seek.

Dignified behavior also appears in King's writings when he describes nonviolent action, often in more pedestrian ways than those Gandhi describes. For instance, he relates a story of a cook in a white household who is confronted during the Montgomery Bus Boycott and asked whether she was participating in it. " 'Oh, no, ma'am, I won't have anything to do with that boycott thing,' the cook said. 'I am just going to stay away from the buses as long as that trouble is going on.' No doubt she left a satisfied audience. But as she walked home from her job, on feet already weary from a full day's work, she walked proudly, knowing that she was marching with a movement that would bring into being nonsegregated bus travel in Montgomery."[18]

We might think of dignified behavior in nonviolence as not only concerned with assent and refusal but also and more broadly with acting like a model for oneself and for others, of conceiving one's actions as exemplifying a vision of what a human being can and perhaps ought to be. Dignified behavior, in this sense, seeks to instantiate in one's behavior what might be called a certain *nobility* of humanity, a nobility that is potentially there but often either not recognized or not acted upon. We do not need to think of this nobility as embodying *all* that is good or potentially good in human beings. After all, writing poetry or climbing mountains or coming to peace with oneself are all good activities for human beings, even if they are not displays of dignity in the sense we're describing here. That is why I referred to dignified behavior as instantiating a *certain* nobility, rather than nobility itself.

This certain nobility of dignified behavior, the behavior displayed in nonviolence, is above all public. It exemplifies a way of being that is in interaction with others but is also, and more important for the moment, before others – in front of them. Since nonviolence is often a public activity, it involves one's being on display, being seen by others. (And even where one is not on display, as with letter-writing in support of a nonviolent campaign, the words one writes or more generally the results of one's behavior is often on display, when it becomes part of the public realm.) In displaying oneself before others, one enacts a way of being that models for them a vision of how political discourse and behavior can occur. It points toward a possible way in which political disagreement can be negotiated, not by anticipating it but instead by making it one's own.

The radical nature of this negotiation should not be understated. It cuts a path between two more traditional ways of understanding how to negotiate political conflict. The first relies on the efficacy of dialogue. On this understanding, the way to resolve political conflict is through discussion in which each side presents its position, offers reasons to the other side, and through the exchange of reasons the best position emerges. We might think of this as the "marketplace of ideas" approach. The weakness of this approach is obvious: political resolution almost never takes place this way. The existence of hierarchies and power relations renders such an approach at best a marginal one. It would be a better world if this were the commonly accepted approach to political conflict. However, we do not live in that world.

The other approach might be seen as a reaction to the naivete of the first one. It lies in the idea that political conflict is resolved simply through the mobilization of superior power on one side in order to silence the other. Here there is no dialogue; there are simply winners and losers. This is a much more cynical view of the negotiation of political conflict, but one that also more accurately describes how conflict is often managed in our world than the first one. Its drawbacks are obvious. First, the silencing of a competing position does not mean it is mistaken. Repression is not refutation. Therefore, the conflict is not so much resolved as simply declared in favor of one side. Second, silencing itself is morally suspect. Among the ways to resolve disagreement, rendering the opponent speechless is rarely to be commended as a defensible approach.

Nonviolent action, as an expression of dignified behavior, seeks to navigate between these two approaches. It rejects the naivete of the first approach by recognizing that at times confrontational or even coercive political action is necessary. And it rejects the second by refusing to silence the opposition. This navigation occurs in a particular way, through a modeling of the behavior that is appropriate to negotiate political conflict. Bondurant writes, in her discussion of Gandhi, that "If the dichotomy between ends and means is logically tenable, the most acute problem for social and political thought is their reconciliation in the field of action ... Nowhere is the problem of means and ends more serious than in the consideration of the conduct of conflict. Political thought has, on the whole, ignored the central problem of means – the development of a technique of action which, in the hands of individual members of a society, can be sued for the constructive resolution of conflict."[19] In her view, Gandhian nonviolence is a way, perhaps a privileged one, of resolving the conflict of means and ends.

My claim here is that nonviolence in general does this through the mechanism of dignified behavior. It does so through modeling a way of negotiating such conflict, recognizing that certain conflicts cannot be resolved through discussion but must not be resolved through silencing. Nonviolence, in this sense, echoes the cliché of many modern movements that we've already twice invoked: be the change you want to see. Dignified behavior is precisely the attempt to be that change. It is an attempt to embody political change in situations of conflict rather than imposing it. In that sense, it seeks to resolve the problem of means and ends through enacting as a means the kinds of ends it envisions, and doing so without neglecting the necessity of coercion where conversion becomes impossible.

We can see examples of dignified behavior across the spectrum of cases we have discussed so far. In the Estonian resistance it occurs at several levels. First, there are the protests themselves. Recall the remarkable demonstration of August 23, 1989 in which two million people joined hands across Estonia, Latvia, and Lithuania to protest against Soviet rule. On the one hand, the protest was a demonstration of dissent against an oppressive empire. On the other hand, however, it was an act of solidarity among peoples, a demonstration (in both senses of the term) of commonality among those who stand unarmed before this empire across national boundaries. The demonstration displayed a way of being in which each person counted as a link in the chain while at the same time seeing every other person as an equally important link in the same chain. Otherwise put, the participants displayed the dignified behavior of defying without attempting the (impossible) task of silencing the adversary and at the same time recognizing the dignity of others who were doing the same.

Dignified behavior appears in several other places in the Estonian resistance movement, and in all of them it provides a vision of how to navigate political conflict. Unique, perhaps, is in the singing involved in this Singing Revolution. The singing of "Land of My People, Land that I Love" was a collective expression of attachment to a history and a culture, not an attempt to silence others. It provided a way of confronting the occupying Soviet authorities through the beauty of song (Estonian culture emphasizes the importance of music in general and singing in particular) rather than any denigration of others. The film *The Singing Revolution* displays the emotional power of tens of thousands of people singing a forbidden song alongside one another, as well as the way the Soviet authorities were nonplussed as to how to respond to what was, after all, a display of national dignity whose character seemed at once to challenge nothing and everything.

We can also see dignified behavior appear in the formation of an alternative government, a step that is often taken in struggles against occupation, both violent and nonviolent. (The movie *The Battle of Algiers* provides an example of the formation of parallel institutions in a violent anti-occupation struggle, in this case the Algerian resistance to French occupation.) Alternative governments or at least parallel institutions provide outlets for democratic decision-making and cultural expression under conditions in which the formal institutions are repressive of rather than responsive to the population. Even where the decisions arrived at by the governments or institutions (for example, policy decisions or marriage licenses) remain unrecognized by occupying government, participation in them offers a vision of – as well as practice in – the sustaining of a democratic collective life. The dignity of behavior lies in the participation itself, in creating alongside others a type of action in which the ends are reflected in the means. After all, if the goal is democratic self-governance, then one can hardly do better in attempting to attain it than in creating and practicing forms of democratic self-governance.

Finally, and perhaps most important, the Estonian struggle displayed a dignity of behavior in its confrontation with the Russian-based Interfront in the trespassing against the alternative Estonian parliament in May 1990. This was the siege in which Interfront members surrounded the building occupied by the alternative government and replanted the Soviet hammer-and-sickle flag after the parliament declared it "illegal." When it looked as though Interfront might storm the building, a call went out over the radio to ethnic Estonians, who in turn surrounded the Interfront members, well outnumbering them. Without an avenue of escape in a situation in which they had threatened the alternative government and sought to reinforce Soviet rule, there could easily have been violence. But in this moment of taut political conflict, the ethnic Estonians surrounding Interfront offered them safe passage away from the parliament building. This move exemplified both a display of dignified behavior in the face of the temptation to suppress those one has in one's power and a way of negotiating political conflict in which the ends (peaceful coexistence) are already instantiated in the means. This is not to say that harmonious coexistence has been achieved between ethnic Estonians and ethnic Russians. As the first chapter noted, it has not. However, dignified behavior during the anti-occupation struggle at least pointed toward ways in which the difficulties of such coexistence might not be worsened.

Another example of dignified behavior as a reconciliation of means and ends worth pausing over is that of the decision-making procedure developed at the New York Occupy and then adopted in Occupy movements in other cities. This was the formation of decision-making by the General Assembly in which each speakers' words were repeated by others so that everyone could hear, and hand signals were created for agreement, disagreement, blocking, points of order, etc., all in the service of trying to make decisions through consensus rather than through voting. A procedure like this, or any consensus procedure, is a delicate operation. The threat to the procedure is that, since it requires everyone's agreement in order to ratify a decision, someone who is obstinate can block any or even every motion. This is what my former student described to me as happening in the Los Angeles Occupy. He said that no motion could be passed because there were particular people who would block it. In fact, it was the same people who were blocking all the motions. The student wondered whether these people were planted by the police in order to undermine the occupation itself.

If such paralysis is to be avoided in a consensus procedure, those who are participating must develop a sense of when to object and when to go along. There may be certain dangers so important that they require blocking a potential consensus, but they are probably few and far between. And we all know, having participated in meetings during the course of our lives, that when people start espousing a position they sometimes become attached to it, and it becomes difficult to get them either to see the other side or to let it go in favor of consensus – or just plain moving on to the next item on the agenda. It requires a certain self-discipline to step back from one's own position in order to ask whether it matters much that that position is adopted. And part of developing that self-discipline lies in recognizing that others too have a viewpoint, one that might be different from one's own but is probably not unreasonable in its own right. This is the self-development that Mark Lance refers to in the article cited in the first chapter, "Fetishizing Process."

The development of the kind of self-discipline that allows one to remove oneself from the immediacy of one's commitment to a position in order to ask about the appropriateness of imposing it can probably be had in many ways. One can engage in mental exercises to step back from one's beliefs, or it can happen with the assistance of others. In New York Occupy there were people who had been involved in anarchist organizations where consensus decisions were the norm who helped train people in techniques of participation in such decisions procedures. However it is arrived at, though, the self-discipline involved allows one to navigate collective space with a certain humility that does not shade over into self-denial. Specifically in the case of New York Occupy, it allowed one to participate alongside others in a process that respected all of its participants not only because it was a consensus process but also because those involved in it participated with respectfulness. Or, to put the point another way, the development of the self-discipline to participate in the consensus process at Occupy was a training in dignified behavior. As we saw earlier, the journalist Todd Gitlin commented, "Occupy's nonviolence was style, a self-presentation, but it was more than a performance ... It ran deeper, expressing some inner conviction, a sense of dignity that people reached in this movement, some sense that they were, whether taken one at a time or *en masse*, inviolable."

This training in dignified behavior is bound to Occupy as a *prefiguring* of a better society. It is a way of seeking to "be the change you want to see." If a better society is going to be developed, it cannot happen solely on the basis of better processes. As the Los Angeles Occupy – or any number of other failed progressive campaigns – have shown, processes alone are not enough to guarantee flourishing. Those involved in the process must jettison the kinds of behavior inculcated in the social arrangements they are rejecting – often individualist and self-serving – in favor of more dignified behavior, behavior that not only seeks to change social arrangements but also seeks to embody those changes within oneself. A better society will be composed not only of better arrangements of power, resources, and opportunities; it will also be composed of people who are better because they are not corrupted – or, more realistically, not *as* corrupted – by the motivations and incentives characteristic of the social arrangements they seek to overcome. This requires the kind of dignified behavior characteristic of nonviolence.

We have seen, then, two sides of dignity valued in nonviolence: the dignity to be respected in others, which is related to but distinct from Kant's conception of dignity, and the dignified behavior required of participants in nonviolence. As we noted earlier, Rosen saw a bond between two of the four strands he isolated in the history of dignity. There is dignity as status (a strand that we have not discussed because it is a more archaic conception that is not relevant to nonviolence), dignity as inherent value, dignity as dignified behavior, and dignity as respectfulness. Moreover, Rosen claimed that "the third strand examined, the idea of dignity as behavior that is dignified, reveals a fourth: a perspective on dignity from which to treat someone *with dignity* is to treat them with respect. Instead of respecting dignity by respecting a set of fundamental rights, dignity requires respectfulness." We are now in a position to see the relation of the third to the fourth by recognizing that the respectfulness characteristic of the fourth strand is a respectfulness of the dignity of the other's inherent value that is the character of the second strand. That recognition is implicit in our discussion of dignified behavior.

To act in a dignified manner, to exhibit dignity, is not something one does alone, particularly in the context of nonviolence. In nonviolence, one's dignified behavior arises in a context of solidarity with some people and conflict with others. Therefore, dignified behavior will be not only *displayed before* others but occur *in interaction* with them. Dignified behavior in interaction with others is behavior that respects the dignity of others in the sense of dignity we defined in the second chapter. It is a respect, or in Rosen's term "respectfulness," of the inherent value of the other, an inherent value that is wider than Kant's autonomy but has affinities with it. Dignified behavior must be behavior in accordance with the recognition that others have lives to lead and that one cannot act, even if one is acting coercively, in such a way as to violate that recognition. So dignified behavior (third strand) requires respectfulness (fourth strand) of the dignity of others (second strand).

We can see this weaving together of the strands of dignity if we turn once again to the cases of the Estonian revolution and Occupy. In Estonia, the protests, in order to be nonviolent, had to be conducted in a way that did not violate the dignity of the Soviet authorities. Moreover, in response to the threats from Interfront, particularly at the Estonian parliament building, a form of confrontation had to emerge that was at once coercive and respectful of the dignity of those who sought to undermine the revolution. The confrontation was coercive in that it made clear to Interfront that it could not take over the parliament building with impunity; and yet by offering the protestors safe exit there was a recognition that it was the actions of Interfront, not the people themselves, that were being opposed.

One might even argue that the singing in this Singing Revolution was dignified behavior, not so much in regard to the Estonians' Soviet adversaries but with one another. It was a way of being with one another that was respectful of the tradition of Estonian singing, the longing for Estonian statehood, and the kinds of solidarity that singing could elicit. This would be an example of what might be called "internal" respectfulness of one's comrades as opposed to the "external" respectfulness of one's adversary. A clearer example of this "internal" respectfulness, however, would be the process by which the General Assemblies of the Occupy movement were operated. When one attempts to hear others by repeating their words (the mic check), listening to alternative points of view, learning when to lay one's own views aside in favor of the collective, etc., one is developing a repertoire of dignified behavior in interaction with those around one. We need not romanticize the Occupy movement here. There were, to be sure, all kinds of internal difficulties and tensions. It is not a question of achieving the status of a collective characterized by purely dignified interactions. Rather, it is a matter of the more and the less. What Occupy sought among its members, and achieved to one extent or another depending on the particular situation, was a vision of how to interact politically with one's peers that respected the diversity of viewpoints among them and the differences that might have led to that diversity.

We might say, then, that in nonviolence dignity as a value is a two-sided coin. On one side is the dignity to be respected by nonviolence and on the other is the dignified behavior that respects it. The two sides of the coin, then, are self (where the self can be an individual or a collective) and other (where the other might be, but is not necessarily, the adversary). Nonviolence is a respectful expression of dignity.

As such, nonviolence displays another characteristic, one that is implied by its two-sided dignity but is not reducible to it. By recognizing the dignity of the other and displaying dignified behavior toward the other, a nonviolent campaign (or a participant in one) treats the other not only as valuable, but as equally valuable to oneself. One presupposes in one's actions the equal dignity of all people, whether on one's own side, the other side, or neither. It is not just dignity, then, that is an inherent value in nonviolent action. Alongside dignity and intertwined with it, equality is a value embraced by nonviolence. It is to that other value, equality, that we must now turn our attention.

5

The Values of Nonviolence: Equality

Equality is often thought of as a political view, in contrast to dignity, which is considered an ethical value. As we saw in the previous chapter, however, nonviolence does not hew to this distinction, for two related reasons. First, nonviolence seeks to be an ethical form of political action. Second, nonviolence rejects the "top-down" approach of traditional political philosophy in application to its own way of operating. This is not to say that nonviolence rejects all top-down approaches, but rather that nonviolence itself must be understood on a "bottom-up" model. As we will see, this makes equality at once an ethical and political concept in nonviolent action.

However, in order to understand the way equality operates in nonviolence, it is worth pausing over its operation in traditional political theory. Equality, alongside freedom or liberty, has been a guiding concept in the contractarian thought we referred to in the previous chapter. Different contractarian theories endorse different types and ranges of equality, but equality plays an important role in almost all of them. In fact, the contemporary theorist Amartya Sen, who has offered his own original theory of contractarianism, insisted that "a common characteristic of virtually all the approaches to the ethics of social arrangements that have stood the test of time is to want equality of *something* – something that has an important place in the particular theory."[1] (Note that he refers to the *ethics* of social arrangements;

however, his reference is still in political theory, since it concerns the justice of broader social arrangements rather than on-the-ground interpersonal interactions.)

Some readers will balk at Sen's characterization, since there are a group of political theories, often known collectively as libertarianism, that seem to allow for vast inequalities in the name of protecting liberty. For libertarians – and we will see momentarily that Kant himself has certain affinities with them – it is liberty or freedom that is to be protected or sustained. According to the libertarian we cannot, for instance, justifiably redistribute wealth through taxation in the name of greater equality, because that would be an infringement on the freedom of the wealth owner. However, Sen's characterization of equality does not eliminate libertarianism from the group of theories that "have stood the test of time." As Sen would characterize it, what libertarians endorse is still equality, but it is equality of freedom from constraint rather than, say, equality of resources or wealth or access to certain goods. We might distinguish libertarian thought from other kinds of political theory by saying that political theorists who endorse equality of resources or wealth or access are more *egalitarian* than libertarianism is, if we recognize that egalitarianism is only one type – or rather a group of types – of equality in the sense that Sen uses that latter term.

When traditional political theory discusses equality (or, in many cases egalitarianism), it does so from a particular angle. It is the equality granted to the citizens (or those who are covered by the social contract) that is at stake. In other words, the question for traditional political theory is, what kind of equality do people in a society deserve, or alternatively, to what kind of equality should they have access? This is a top-down question. It is a question of what the state or its institutions should protect or nourish or foster. It is not a question of how people should act toward one another, which is considered to be an ethical rather than political question. Instead, it is a question regarding how the formal political institutions of a society should be constructed, that is, what principles should guide their construction. As we will see, the equality – and more specifically the egalitarianism – of nonviolence does not operate in this way but rather asks about the equality which is presupposed in nonviolent action.

In keeping with the approach of the previous chapter, it would be worth starting this discussion with a contrast case. Moreover, Kant's political thought offers an instructive case, since he seeks to construct a political thought that reflects his ethical commitment to the categorical imperative. Simplifying a bit, one might say that the animating question for Kant's political thought is one of how to construct a political order that protects the dignity of individuals, which for Kant is their ability to act in accordance with the categorical imperative.

Kant's own view of politics is more libertarian than egalitarian. His political concerns, especially in his founding political work *Metaphysics of Morals*, center on the preservation of freedom, which Kant seems to see as largely a matter of freedom from coercion. "Right," he tells us, "is therefore the sum of the conditions under which the choice of one can be united with the choice of another in accordance with a universal law of freedom."[2] With this thought, Kant seeks to align his politics with his ethics. We might put the alignment roughly this way: that freedom is the supposition that must be thought to be the character of beings inasmuch as we take them as rational. This is because freedom is the ability to act rationally as opposed to being controlled by one's instincts and desires. To act rationally is, as we saw in the previous chapter, to act in accordance with the categorical imperative. Therefore, a political system of rational beings must be a system that preserves the conditions of freedom, that is, the conditions under which it is possible for rational beings to act rationally, which of course is nothing other than the ability to follow the categorical imperative. Fundamental to that preservation is noninterference with action.

This condition of choice can be preserved under a number of different political regimes, and there is nothing in the *Metaphysics of Morals* that would militate toward an egalitarian as opposed to hierarchical form of government as the ground of preservation of choice. Kant's preferred orientation in that text is for a constitutional form of government, one that has more affinity with the liberal tradition than with the nonviolent resistance campaigns with which we are currently concerned. This is not to say that nonviolent campaigns necessarily oppose constitutional forms of government. Particularly in cases where those campaigns oppose autocratic governments, such as in Egypt or the Philippines, the *goal* might be to create a liberal or constitutional government. The point here is that in its operation, a nonviolent campaign does not work constitutionally. It works instead through a certain kind of "bottom-up" egalitarianism.

What I am going to propose here, however, is that if we accept something broadly like Kant's categorical imperative with respect to people, particularly as it is found in the second and third formulations of the categorical imperative, then we should look toward a more egalitarian view of politics. In other words, a Kantian ethics opens out much more clearly onto an egalitarian politics than a constitutional or liberal one. Or, to put the point another way, Kant's conception of dignity is one that sits more comfortably with the kind of egalitarianism characteristic of nonviolence than it does with the "top-down" political thought characteristic of the liberal tradition. To be precise, this is not to say that there is no connection between his ethics and liberal political thought, but rather that the relation between his ethical commitments and the kind of politics practiced by nonviolence is more seamless. And the reason it is more seamless has to do with the egalitarianism implicit in his ethical thought, a thought that – as we have already seen – gives a political character to dignity when pressed into the service of nonviolence.

Let us recall briefly Kant's second and third formulations of the categorical imperative. The second formulation reads, "Act in such a way that you always treat humanity, whether in your own person or in the person of any other, never simply as a means but always at the same time as an end."[3] And the third formulation calls for rational beings to act in accordance with a kingdom of ends, a kingdom being defined as "a systematic union of different rational beings under common laws."[4] We know that to treat someone as an end rather than simply as a means is to treat them as having intrinsic value. But it is to do more than that. For why does one treat them as having intrinsic value? Or better, what is the intrinsic value that forms the ground on which to act toward them? For Kant it is, as we have seen, rationality, and specifically the kind of rationality that allows one to follow the categorical imperative. A rational being is to be treated not merely as a means but also as an end. Moreover, for Kant, rationality is not a matter of degree. One has it, or one does not. The implication here is that all those who possess rationality possess it in *equal measure* in this particular sense.

Rational beings are in something akin to, although not exactly, what the philosopher Wilfrid Sellars would call "the space of reasons." For Sellars, humans occupy the space of reasons in the sense that we can give reasons to one another for what we believe as well as understand the reasons given by others. This seems obvious, but there is more to it than meets the eye. The space of reasons is a social space. It is not that I have my reasons and you have your reasons and that sometimes they happen to meet. Rather, the space of reasons is a space we are born into and occupy together, and in our conversation we navigate through it. We might think of it as an inferential space, a space where, from being committed to certain beliefs, other commitments follow. (For example, from the fact that I believe an object is red, I am committed to believing that it is colored, that it is not blue, etc.)

For Sellars, the space of reasons is not a static space. It is not as though there are reasons and their inferential connections out there and that we just have to figure out what they are. Instead, the space of reasons is dynamic and changing. Based on the reason to believe one thing, we might wind up questioning something else that we used to believe or that many other people believe. However, we cannot divorce that questioning or that challenging from the space of reasons itself. There is no place outside the space of reasons from which we can challenge something inside it. Because to challenge a belief within the network of reasons that is currently accepted, we must have a reason to do so. And that reason, in turn, must be one that people can believe, based on their other beliefs. So any adequate challenge to what people believe must come from within the space of reasons that we all occupy. As Sellars puts the point, " 'empirical knowledge, like its sophisticated extension, science, is rational, not because it has a *foundation* but because it is a self-correcting enterprise which can put *any* claim in jeopardy, though not *all* at once."[5]

So the space of reasons is a dynamic and changing but not, for all that, an arbitrary space. It is a space occupied by beings capable of rationality. And, following Kant, if one is to be

treated as having intrinsic value on the basis of one's rationality, one is to be treated – and to treat others – as equally
possessed of such value. That is to say that one is to see others
as having intrinsic value equal to oneself, since the intrinsic
value one has on the basis of which one is to be treated as
an end is equal to that of other rational beings.

This thought leads naturally into Kant's idea of a kingdom
of ends. If everyone possesses rationality to the same extent,
or better if rationality is a binary category and so precludes
the idea of extent, then every rational being is to be treated
as an end. A society in which the categorical imperative was
generally followed would be a union of beings each of whom
treated all the others as ends. And, if we take the term
"common laws" in a broad sense to refer to the ways these
rational beings agree to live together, then the kingdom of
ends is a society of rational beings treating one another
equally inasmuch as they are all rational beings. Finally, since
it is rationality that is at issue in matters of ethics, we might
put this point by saying that, from the standpoint of ethics,
the kingdom of ends is one in which everyone treats everyone
else as an equal, that is, a moral equal.

For Kant, as we have seen, the political implication of
treating one another as equals is the preservation of freedom
negatively defined, that is, as freedom from interference.
However, one might raise the question of whether in fact the
preservation of negative freedom is the best expression of
treating one another as having intrinsic value or as co-mem-
bers of a kingdom of ends. Does the more libertarian idea of
preserving a freedom from interference as a way of allowing
people to act upon the categorical imperative capture the
operation of the categorical imperative in social relations
better than another, more egalitarian approach would? We
have seen from our brief discussion of Sellars that the space
of reasons is a social one. Might it be that in capturing the
social character of the space of reasons we might want to
think of the political character of the categorical imperative
not as a matter of isolated individuals acting on its basis but
instead in an egalitarian way in which everyone considers
everyone else an equal partner? In order to begin to address
this question, we should turn to a contemporary French
thinker, Jacques Rancière. Rancière has thought long and

hard about equality and its relation to politics and especially political campaigns.

In 1989, Rancière published a book entitled *The Ignorant Schoolmaster*. It is a biography of a French revolutionary, Joseph Jacotot, who flees to Belgium after the Restoration in France. He is hired as a teacher of French in a Flemish area in Belgium. Unfortunately, he does not speak Flemish. This pedagogical lack, however, does not deter him. Jacotot teaches his students from a bilingual text of *Telemachus*, having them follow along in Flemish while he teaches from the French. Eventually, he gives the students assignments on *Telemachus*, to be done in French, with only this bilingual edition as a reference point. As it happens, the students perform in ways that are not only passable, but indeed superior. Jacotot decides, for this reason and several others, that people are equally intelligent. The pedagogical problem to be overcome is not, in his view, that of intelligence but rather that of attention. If students are willing to attend to the material, they, or at least most of them, will be able to grasp it.

Jacotot tests this assumption by teaching courses he doesn't know anything about, such as painting and law. He figures that if people are equally intelligent, they do not need him to delineate the material for them, and so they should be able to learn something he doesn't know. As with the French course, the students excel in their various studies. With this, Jacotot believes that he has evidence that people are equally intelligent.

Rancière is not particularly interested in the question of what Jacotot has or has not proved, which is probably a good thing, since we're not all likely to sign on to the idea of equal intelligence based on Jacotot's pedagogical experiments. Instead, Rancière writes, "[O]ur problem isn't proving that all intelligence is equal. It's seeing what can be done under that presupposition. And for this, it's enough for us that the opinion be possible – that is, that no opposing truth be proved."[6] For Rancière, what is interesting in Jacotot's story is not the evidence he might have provided for the view that everyone is equally intelligent, which, after all, is pretty thin. It is instead the experiment itself. It is the idea that one might act, and perhaps act successfully, presupposing the equal intelligence of others.

What might this equal intelligence consist in? We will investigate this further as things unfold, but might define it initially as the ability to construct a meaningful life alongside and in interaction with others. Or, to put the point in a Sellarsian fashion, it would be the ability to inhabit the space of reasons in regard to the creation of one's life. Now this way of putting things might seem a bit individualistic. One could wonder whether the ability to inhabit that space of reasons in regard to my own life would give me any purchase on social interaction. However, we should recall the earlier point that the Sellarsian space of reasons is not a private space but indeed a social one. To be immersed in it is to be able to engage in reflection and thought that one will share with others who inhabit that space. When Rancière asks what can be done under the presupposition of equal intelligence, I take it that something like this is the equal intelligence he is presupposing. And when he asks *what can be done* under this presupposition, he is interested not in proving it but rather in what might happen if we treat one another this way.

We will soon turn to the political implications of that presupposition, which is the arena in which Rancière ultimately sets it to work. Before turning there, however, it is worth lingering for a moment over the affinities between Rancière's presupposition of equality and Kant's view of freedom. This will prove important when we turn to Rancière's politics (and then to nonviolence), because for Rancière the presupposition of equality is what a democratic politics expresses, just as for Kant politics preserves freedom first and foremost. As Kant tells us, "*Freedom* (independence from being constrained by another's choice), insofar as it can coexist with the freedom of every other in accordance with a universal law, is the only original right belonging to every man in virtue of his humanity."[7] The affinities between Kant and Rancière can be drawn on two levels.

The first level is structural. That is to say, freedom for Kant and equal intelligence for Rancière occupy analogous places in their respective thought. Both of them offer their concepts as presuppositions rather than as evidence or proof. For Kant, of course, freedom is the presupposition that must exist in order for someone to be considered a rational being, that is, a being capable of conforming his or her actions to the requirements of the categorical imperative. Freedom, Kant writes in the *Groundwork of the Metaphysic of Morals*, "is a mere Idea: its objective validity can in no way be exhibited by reference to laws of nature and consequently freedom can never admit of full comprehension ... It holds only as a necessary presupposition of reason in a being who believes himself to be conscious of a will."[8] This is because, for Kant, we can never prove that freedom exists. It doesn't show itself to us in the empirical world. We must act as though other human beings were free, possessed of a will over which they have some control – and thus capable of following the categorical imperative – but we can never demonstrate in a scientific way that such freedom actually exists.

Rancière's approach to equal intelligence is also one of presupposition rather than demonstration. It is not a necessary presupposition in the same way Kant's is; however, we might call it a necessary presupposition in another way. For Rancière, democratic politics, or what he sometimes simply calls politics, is defined as action under the presupposition of equality. He writes, in a passage whose complexity we will unfold momentarily, "I ... propose to reserve the term *politics* for an extremely determined activity antagonistic to policing: whatever breaks with the tangible configuration whereby parties and parts or lack of them are defined by a presupposition that, by definition, has no place in that configuration – that of the part that has no part ... political activity is always a mode of expression that undoes the perceptible divisions of the police order by implementing a basically heterogeneous assumption, that of the part who have no part, an assumption that, at the end of the day, itself demonstrates the contingency of the order, the equality of any speaking being with any other speaking being."[9] We will return to the concept of policing below, but let us note for the moment that, in Rancière's view, we all live in police orders, and those orders operate hierarchically, that is, on the presupposition not of the equality but of the inequality of people's intelligence. In order for a democratic politics to take place, then, it is necessary to presuppose the equal intelligence of what Rancière calls all "speaking beings."

We might mark the limits of the structural analogy between these two presuppositions by noting that while both function as the central conceptual presuppositions of their political thought, for Kant the presupposition functions transcendentally while for Rancière it functions performatively.[10] Transcendental conditions are usually taken to be the metaphysical conditions of possibility for something's existence or its appearing in the way that it does. A performative presupposition, by contrast, might be defined as a presupposition on which people act that makes something appear the way that it does; it arises not out of some metaphysical condition but out of a particular performance.

For Kant the presupposition of freedom is a condition for the possibility of taking a rational being to be rational. That is, one cannot think of a being as rational without necessarily supposing that it is free. This is because without the presupposition of freedom, people will not so much act rationally as they will on the basis of pure causality – like machines rather than rational beings. By contrast, for Rancière, the presupposition of equal intelligence is not so much that it allows us to consider people to be capable of rationality – or in Rancière's case, a democratic politics – as it allows such a politics to get off the ground. The presupposition of equal intelligence is what grounds the performance of politics, not merely the assumption of its ability to be performed.

It is true that Kant also seeks to ground particular political orders, inasmuch as they are just, on his own necessary presupposition of freedom. That is the point of the *Metaphysics of Morals*. And in that sense, there seems to be a performative aspect to his thought. Moreover, although we cannot pursue this point here, one might interpret the positing of certain beings as rational to be performative itself. In the end, though, for Kant the grounding of political orders is deduced from the character of rationality, however situated, rather than, as with Rancière, performed from the activity of asking where and how far we might go with the presupposition of equal intelligence.

In addition to the structural analogy of the two concepts, they share a certain similarity of content, although again they are not identical. For Kant, freedom, at the ethical level, is a certain capacity. It is the capacity to act in accordance with the categorical imperative. In the *Metaphysics of Morals*, Kant insists that, "Only freedom in relation to the internal lawgiving of reason is really a capacity; the possibility of deviating from it is an incapacity."[11] Likewise, for Rancière, equal intelligence is a certain capacity. It is the capacity to make decisions for oneself through what Jacotot would call "attention" and Sellars an engagement in the "space of reasons," a capacity one shares with others and can recognize oneself as sharing with others. It is the capacity that one presupposes if one is to take part in the ordering of collective life rather than having that life ordered for one by the work of the as yet undefined *police*. In both cases, the concept brought into play to ground politics is a capacity for choice: in one case choice of the moral law and in the other case choice of participating in the character of collective living.

The upshot of this is that Rancière's presupposition of equal intelligence is structurally and substantively similar to that of Kant's freedom. Now, structural similarities do not display convergences of thought. The point at this stage is a smaller one. Kant sees the preservation of a presupposed freedom as the central principle of any political philosophy. Freedom is the ability to act in accordance with the moral law, the categorical imperative. The moral law prescribes treating others as ends and not simply as means and envisioning a community as a kingdom of ends. Now, what happens if we substitute for the transcendentally grounded concept of freedom a concept of the presupposition of the equality of intelligence? What happens is that we can still preserve the Kantian ethical thread while giving it an arguably more direct political orientation, one that will ultimately lead us to a deeper understanding of the normative character of nonviolence.

To see how, let's hold on to two ideas: the categorical imperative on the one hand and the presupposition of the equality of intelligence as a substitute for freedom on the other. What, then, would the transition from ethics to politics look like? The categorical imperative demands that we treat rational beings as ends rather than simply as means. Here, by rational beings we will mean beings that are equally intelligent in the sense we have discussed. And, in envisioning the kingdom of ends, we will be envisioning a community in which everyone presupposes the equal intelligence of everyone else, again in the sense we have discussed. A political community, then, would be a community in which this ethical framework was sustained by operating on the basis of the presupposition of everyone's equal intelligence.

Now what would that look like? In order to answer this question, we need to remain clear about what is being presupposed by equal intelligence. Rancière is not claiming that equal intelligence requires that we all can understand quantum physics or string theory. The presupposition of equal intelligence, in Rancière's handling of it, is a political concept. It implies that all of us, unless we are somehow damaged emotionally or intellectually, can envision meaningful lives for ourselves and sort out to one extent or another with others how to carry out or conduct those lives. We don't need anyone, particularly anyone in a position of political authority, to dictate to us what a good life would be or how to we ought to go about creating our lives. We can figure that out for ourselves alongside, rather than beneath or above, others. *Alongside others* implies that we are not alone, and that we can make mistakes. But those mistakes can be pointed out to us; they need not be forced upon us by a social or political authority.

Before proceeding any further, let us step back a bit to see how the ideas in this chapter intersect with those we have already seen in regard to nonviolence. Recall once again the concept of dignity that is respected by nonviolence: the having of a human life to lead, more specifically *the ability to engage in projects and relationships that unfold over time; to be aware of one's death in a way that affects how one sees the arc of one's life; to have biological needs like food, shelter, and sleep; to have basic psychological needs like care and a sense of attachment to one's surroundings.* Nonviolence must respect this, not in the sense that it cannot, for instance, interfere in anyone else's projects – or else Mubarak would still be President of Egypt and Marcos would never have left the Philippines. As we have seen, nonviolence can be coercive. Rather, one must respect the fact that other human beings have projects, etc., and not treat them as though they didn't or that, for instance, their having projects is less worthy than one's own having projects. This is the broadened idea of dignity discussed in the previous chapter, and it corresponds to a broadened conception of the categorical imperative as respecting the dignity of others.

In the convergence between this broadened idea of the categorical imperative and the presupposition of equal intelligence, two related elements have been added. We may see them as implicit in the discussion of the previous chapter, but Rancière's ideas bring them to the surface. They are the social context in which dignity is to be respected and the equality of dignity. The first emerges when we modify the Kantian conception of reasons with Sellars' notion of the space of reasons. For Kant, reason might be thought of as a monolith – as Reason rather than just reason or reasons. To act in accordance with the categorical imperative is to act in accordance with a pre-existing Reason. In fact, for Kant, violations of the categorical imperative bring one into contradiction with one's own will. Lying, as we saw, cannot be in accordance with the categorical imperative because, on the first formulation of the categorical imperative, nobody can will a world in which everyone lied all the time. The reason for this is that if everyone lied, nobody would believe anyone else, and lying would lose its point.

For Kant, then, morality is a relationship between an individual actor and Reason. However, if we suppose that we inhabit a space of reasons rather than of Reason, then reasons become social. They arise within our interaction with others, when we give not only ourselves but also one another reasons to believe, to notice, to desire, to wish, to fear, to enthuse over, or to do any number of things. Reasons are the webs of inferential connections that suffuse our social practices. They exist not in an individual's relationship to a timeless monolith of Reason but in our evolving relationships with one another.

Among the implications of this is that each of us has a finite relationship to reasons, which is especially important when it comes to normative issues of how one should act or what kind of society people should live in. If, in the Kantian style, we think we can deduce a proper set of moral obligations and then a political arrangement from a timeless Reason, then inasmuch as we are in contact with the Reason, we are infallible. Others who disagree with us are simply wrong. However, if we adopt the Sellarsian view of a space of reasons, then it is always possible that we are mistaken or that another person is seeing something we do not. We must adopt a certain modesty with respect to our own beliefs, and a certain openness to the beliefs of those with whom we disagree.

We have seen this idea in another context in Gandhi's discussion of Truth. Recall from the third chapter that, for Gandhi, nobody ever corners the market on Truth. This is one of the sources of nonviolence for him. If none of us has a privileged access to Truth, then we must adopt an attitude of *ahimsa* – nonviolence – toward others. One must attempt first of all to persuade others of one's own position, recognizing that it could be oneself that is mistaken. Of course, persuasion may fail, and the other may have to be coerced; and, as we have seen, even the persuasion of moral jiu-jitsu may not convince the adversary. However, nonviolence, even when coercive, respects the fact the adversary is a member of the space of reasons and remains open to whatever aspect of the Truth he or she may have access to. What we can see here is that this openness is grounded not only in a respect for the other but in a view of reasons embedded in our social lives rather than existing in a realm apart.

The social context of reasons is the first element our discussion has added to the normative character of nonviolence. The second is the equality of dignity. This is bound both to the social character of reasons and to Rancière's idea of equal intelligence. For Rancière, the presupposition of a democratic politics is that we are equally able to construct meaningful lives for ourselves. To put it in the terms we have discussed, we are equally capable of living human lives. We may not be equally capable of living specific lives; not everyone among us, for instance, could be a neurosurgeon or astrophysicist. However, we are all capable of reflecting on our lives, developing life plans and projects, and enacting them alongside others. As such, we are all equal in dignity – or at least the presupposition of a democratic politics is that we are all equal in dignity. Equal intelligence in Rancière's sense is nothing more than equal dignity in the second of Rosen's strands, that of inherent value, and requires the third and fourth strands of dignity – dignified behavior and respectfulness – as a proper response.

To presuppose the equality of intelligence in this sense is to presuppose that, in conducting lives together, people can engage in reasoning and discussion with others and can orient themselves in ways that would best allow each to conduct one's life as one sees fit. This does not mean that one can do what one wants. It is not a formula for noninterference. The social character of the space of reasons has the consequence that there will likely be conflicts in the community. There will be disagreements about distribution of goods, allocation of positions, extent and character of particular rights, etc. These conflicts are not solved simply by appeal to a principle of liberty, but rather by discussion and resolution through a process that respects the equal intelligence of everyone involved. My point here is only to emphasize that equality of intelligence is, as a political matter, tied to the question of process rather than to that of a particular distribution or allocation.

We have already seen a process of decision-making that tacitly presupposes the equality of intelligence with the operation of the General Assembly in New York Occupy. In this process, each participant in discussion was deemed equally worthy of being heard. This was guaranteed by the mic check. This equal worthiness does not entail that everyone must agree, only that everyone must take the opinions voiced by others to reflect a viewpoint worth engaging. As we noted earlier, to participate in this process without undermining it requires training in listening to others and in knowing when and where to press one's own view. In light of Rancière's work, we might now re-state that necessity this way: adequate participation in a consensus decision-making process requires each participant to recognize the equal intelligence of the others. This recognition allows discussion to move forward with a lower probability (although, of course, no guarantee) that someone will decide to hijack the process by deciding that his or her viewpoint must always prevail.

With these ideas in mind, we can now turn toward the kind of politics envisioned in Rancière's writings, to see how they develop aspects of nonviolence that we have not yet touched upon. I can only, of course, offer a quick sketch of Rancière's framework here, but I hope it is enough to suggest how his thought of equality is placed within a political context. Rancière contrasts what he calls, borrowing from Michel Foucault's lectures at the Collège de France, the term *police* that we saw earlier, with what he calls *politics*.

"Politics," he writes, "is generally seen as the set of procedures whereby the aggregation and consent of collectivities is
achieved, the organization of powers, the distribution of
places and roles, and the systems for legitimizing this distribution. I propose to give this system of distribution another
name. I propose to call it *the police*."[12] The police, then, are
not the folks in uniforms with truncheons. Rather, the police
is broadly the set of hierarchical distributions and their jus-
tifications characteristic of a particular society. We do not
need to linger over the specifics of this concept, since for our
purposes it stands as the background for the more relevant
concept of the democratic politics Rancière endorses.

Let's recall, then, Rancière's elusive definition of politics.
"I...propose to reserve the term *politics* for an extremely
determined activity antagonistic to policing: whatever breaks
with the tangible configuration whereby parties and parts or
lack of them are defined by a presupposition that, by definition, has no place in that configuration – that of the part that
has no part... political activity is always a mode of expression
that undoes the perceptible divisions of the police order by
implementing a basically heterogeneous assumption, that of
the part who has no part, an assumption that, at the end of
the day, itself demonstrates the contingency of the order, the
equality of any speaking being with any other speaking
being."[13] This, I grant, is a bit of a mouthful. In order to
unpack it, it is worth focusing on the term he uses twice: the
part that has no part.

In any police order, there are various hierarchies. These
hierarchies often differ in different societies, but it is difficult
to find an example of a society without one. There are hierarchies of gender, of race, of sexual orientation, of class, of
religion, of age, etc. One of the central functions of these
hierarchies is to deny participation, or at least equal participation, to those considered to be on the wrong end of the
hierarchy. Putting the matter in different terms, there are
those who are considered by a society as having a part to play
in its direction and maintenance, and those who do not have
a part. In a complex society, such as ours, there is no single
strict division between those who do and do not have a part,
but instead a series of distinct but often overlapping or inter-
secting divisions. These divisions can work in two opposing

directions at the same time, for example with upper-class women who have a part because of their class but in another sense don't because of their gender. Nevertheless these divisions operate by allocating roles that have to do with, in Rancière's terms, having and not having a part.

Politics, then, as he defines it, is a matter of members of a part that has no part in a given police order acting as though they indeed do have a part, acting as though the police order which has not allocated them a part is contingent, or better arbitrary, and indeed unjustified. It is a matter of those who do not have a part presupposing that they are equal to those who do, and acting on the basis of that presupposition. As Rancière puts the point, they act on the presupposition of the equality of any speaking being with any other speaking being.

How might such a politics look? We must note first that one cannot define a politics of equality by speaking of a generic type of action. A strike, a demonstration, a protest of some sort or another, might or might not be an expression of the presupposition of equality. For instance, recent demonstrations of immigrants, both illegal and legal, here in the USA was an example of such politics, particularly among the illegal immigrants, since they acted on the presupposition of their equality with US citizens by publicly demonstrating. Alternatively, a demonstration against, say, equal rights for gays and lesbians would not so much qualify as politics in the Rancièrean sense. It would be operating on the presupposition of *inequality* rather than equality. Whether an act or a campaign is one of such a politics is a matter, then, of interpretation; one has to look at the character of the act or campaign itself. Rancière notes, "Equality is not a given that politics puts into application, an essence incarnated in the law, or a goal that is to be attained. It is only a presupposition that must be discerned in the practices that implement it."[14]

Second, this presupposition is instantiated not in what is offered to people by their governing institutions, which already presupposes a hierarchy between grantor and grantee, but instead by people acting on their own behalf, or in solidarity with those who act on their own behalf. This is where Rancière's politics displays its particular Kantian ethical flavor or at least the Kantian view as we have modified it.

The animating presupposition of equality is one that takes everyone to be equally capable of creating meaningful lives for themselves. Thus, in an act or movement of politics in Rancière's sense, one treats oneself and those around one as equals, as partners rather than as superiors or inferiors. Again, this does not entail that people cannot be wrong in their views. What it entails is the distinction between being mistaken and needing the authority of another. If I am mistaken, this will come out in our conversation or our interactions with one another. If, alternatively, I need the authority of another, it is because I am less capable than the other of getting things right; I am unequal to that other.

What Rancière describes here is convergent with nonviolence as we have come to understand it. In fact, it would seem that Rancière's view must imply nonviolence as a sort of default method. It might not be that a politics arising out of the presupposition of the equality of every speaking being would require a strict adherence to nonviolence. This would only be so if violence were necessarily in conflict with presupposing the equality of the other. Whether this is the case is a vexed question. Whether violence to another can ever be reconciled with the presupposition of the equality of that other is a difficult one to sort out. In some cases, for instance those of self-defense, it might seem possible. But this would require a deeper reflection on violence. For our purposes, the nonviolent *orientation* implied by Rancière's work is enough. His politics seems to necessitate a nonviolent approach as the first and default option.

Let's look at a couple of examples of how the presupposition of equality works in nonviolence. An obvious example of politics as collective action from the presupposition of equality is the lunch counter sit-ins of the Civil Rights movement. Here blacks and whites sat together in the simple activity of ordering lunch at segregated lunch counters. There were, to be sure, requests being made: people, after all, were requesting lunch. However, that request was based upon an action that presupposed that everyone who sat down at a particular lunch counter was equal to everyone else who sat down at that lunch counter. And that presupposition is precisely a broadly Kantian one: it treats everyone as not merely a means but also as an end, it does so by treating everyone equally, and in doing so it acts within a general vision of a kingdom of ends.

One might object here that, in fact, the motivation for the lunch counter sit-ins had nothing to do with the presupposition of equality. Rather, it was a tactic that was used to reveal the inequality suffered by African-Americans in a particularly stark way. The participants in the sit-ins knew that they were going to be reviled and perhaps even attacked. They did not act on the presupposition of equality, then, but instead on a tactical understanding of what was likely to occur. This objection is an important one, because it brings us back to the distinction we first saw in the second chapter between principled and pragmatic nonviolence.

For a principled nonviolence, one must always act nonviolently out of a commitment to respect for the equal dignity of the other. It is not because nonviolence is more effective that one must use it, but because it is nonviolence. Even if nonviolence were less effective than violence, for the proponent of principled nonviolence one must nevertheless remain faithful to its requirements. By contrast, for the pragmatic nonviolent participant, the resort to nonviolence occurs solely because in certain circumstances it is likely to be more effective than violence. Particularly when the adversary is well armed, a campaign of violence is likely to be futile. So nonviolence becomes the best, that is the most practical, political option.

In formulating his ethical view, Kant himself makes almost exactly the same distinction, opting for principle over pragmatics. He argues that in acting morally, one must not only act in accordance with the moral law, but out of respect for it. It is not enough, in his view, to act as the categorical imperative would dictate for reasons of self-interest. One must act as the categorical imperative counsels because it is one's duty to do so. "Love," he tells us, "out of inclination cannot be commanded; but kindness done from duty – although no inclination impels us, and even although natural and unconquerable disinclination stands in our way – is *practical*, and not *pathological*, love, residing in the will and not in the propensions of feeling, in principles of action and not melting compassion; and it is this practical love alone which can be an object of command."[15] (When Kant refers to love out of inclination as pathological, he does not mean mentally unbalanced but rather a love out of pathos – sympathetic feeling for the other.)

We should not think of the presupposition of equality, however, solely in psychological terms. Although mentally presupposing equality would often be a good indicator of the presupposition of equality at work, it can nevertheless be at work even without conscious awareness of it by the actors. That is what Rancière means when he speaks of discerning the presupposition in practices that implement it. Whether an act or a movement operates on the presupposition of equality is a matter of interpretation, and the actors themselves do not have exclusive privilege to decide on that either way. (In fact, those conservative Christians who militate against equal rights for gays and lesbians often couch their arguments in terms of equality, as though homosexuals having equal rights somehow constitutes an oppression of Christian beliefs.) It is open to us, then, and I think it is right, to interpret the lunch counter sit-ins as actions presupposing the equality of everyone regardless of any tactical decisions involved.

This interpretation is in line with the discussion in the second chapter regarding the convergence of principled and pragmatic nonviolence. There I said that in practice, a pragmatic nonviolent campaign is indistinguishable from a principled one. They both *act* on the basis of respect for the dignity of others, even where the pragmatic proponent does not actually possess that respect as a motivation while the principled proponent does. Here the situation is the same. Acting on the presupposition of equality does not require that one believe it. It does not even require that one knows that one is so acting. It is in the acting itself that the presupposition emerges. We might say that in nonviolence the presupposition of equality is enacted whether or not it is considered. Those participating in the lunch counter sit-ins need not have thought about the relation of their actions to the presupposition of equality (although it is likely that many of them thought a lot about equality in some sense); they need only have conducted themselves, against Kant's insistence, in accordance with that presupposition.

Another example of the presupposition of equality at work appears in one of the most famous of all nonviolent campaigns, the Indian Salt Satyagraha of 1930–1. This campaign is a model of nonviolent resistance, and would be worth pausing over for that reason alone. However, it is also a demonstration of the presupposition of equality in action.[16]

The Salt Satyagraha took place in response to the British Salt Acts imposed on India. Those Acts allowed the British a monopoly on salt production in India, to which a tax was added that helped support the colonial occupation of India. According to Bondurant, "Revenue realized from the Salt Tax amounted at this time to $25,000,000 out of a total revenue of about $800,000,000."[17] In addition to its material support of the British occupation, the salt tax created a particular hardship for the poor. There were, then, three important reasons for resisting the Salt Acts. First, and most obvious, they helped fund British imperial ambitions in India. Second, since they were already resented, it would be easy to mobilize the population against them. Third, and related to both of the other reasons, the Salt Acts were a symbol of British occupation: to challenge them was implicitly to challenge the entirety of British rule in India.

The initial stage of the campaign, after appealing to the British government to repeal the Salt Acts and announcing the commitment to civil disobedience, was the famous Salt March. Gandhi and those from his ashram left Ahmedabad on March 12, 1930, determined to march to the sea at Dandi and there illegally and publicly use sea water in order to produce salt. This march, which lasted several weeks, also had the effect of publicizing the campaign and galvanizing local populations along the way. This would be important for the longer term campaign, since the march itself was restricted to closer followers of Gandhi's, who could be trusted to retain nonviolent discipline.

The British reaction to the Salt March was subdued. Officials recognized that if they arrested Gandhi that would backfire on them (a form of political jiu-jitsu), so they refrained. This led to the next stage of the campaign, the attempt to occupy the large British salt works at Dharsana. This move, again announced in advance by Gandhi, was not ignored by the authorities. On May 5, Gandhi was arrested. However, his followers persisted and were joined by others. Much like the Vykom Road Campaign discussed in the third chapter, this persistence took the form of nonviolent attempts to enter the salt works and refusal to respond to attacks by the British police, which were in this case particularly barbarous. The campaign sparked resistance of various types all over India. There were nonpayment of taxes, disobedience of laws restricting opposition, and boycotts of foreign goods. Thus, those who could not participate directly in the attempt to occupy the salt works were able to participate in the campaign, and with the advent of the monsoon season (which, as we saw, created difficulties – and also opportunities – for those in the Vykom Road Campaign) allowed resistance to the Salt Tax to continue even when it was difficult to mobilize people to occupy the salt works. Throughout, Gandhi encouraged nonviolent resistance in the face of British police attacks, even congratulating those who were injured on their commitment and fortitude, writing for instance in the wake of a bullet wound to his colleague Jairamdas Daulatram, "Jairamdas' injury gave me unmixed joy. It is the injury to leaders that would bring relief. The law of sacrifice is uniform throughout the world. To be effective it demands the sacrifice of the bravest and most spotless."[18]

Over the course of 1930 and into 1931, disobedience continued and was exacerbated by British repression. The Salt Satyagraha exhibited political jiu-jitsu to a striking degree, as jailings, beatings, and press censorship only served to stiffen resistance and further undermine the British goals. Finally, in March 1931, Gandhi and the British Viceroy of India Lord Irwin signed an agreement that, while it did not formally overturn the salt laws, reinterpreted them in such a way as to remove their teeth. Specifically, the agreement stated that the British governing body "would extend their administrative provisions, on lines already prevailing in certain places, in order to permit local residents in villages, immediately adjoining areas where salt can be collected or made, to collect or make salt for domestic consumption or sale within such villages, but not for sale to, or trading with, individuals living outside them."[19] In addition, there were provisions to restore confiscated property, give amnesty to jailed nonviolent protestors etc. as well as a promise to include members of Gandhi's Congress Party in discussions for further constitutional reform. In short, the campaign was an unalloyed victory for Gandhi and a model of nonviolent resistance.

The Salt Satyagraha also stands as an example of the presupposition of equality at work. One might balk at the idea that a campaign largely led by a single individual and whose initial participants were restricted to those in his ashram as such an example. However, the presupposition of equality does not require that everyone be allowed to fulfill every role. Such a requirement would undermine the ability of a campaign of nonviolence to count on any division of labor. It would also subvert any process of decision-making by a deliberative body, since any individual could demand that a decision be rescinded in order to allow him or her to occupy another position in a given campaign. To put the point another way, the presupposition of equality is not the presupposition of maximal liberty for individuals. Rather, it is the presupposition that everyone is capable of constructing a life alongside others in ways and along the lines discussed in the second chapter. The presupposition of equality must respect dignity in that sense.

The Salt Satyagraha did this both in its overall conception and in its dynamic unfolding. Regarding overall conception, the local goal was to allow Indians to manufacture and sell their own salt. Of course, they were perfectly capable of doing so, and doing so would enhance their lives, especially the lives of poorer Indians. The campaign reflected this recognition, but did so not only as a demand but, and in a more Rancièrean vein, as an activity. The Salt March did not simply ask that Indians be treated equally to the British when it came to making salt: the marchers *made salt*. Their protest consisted in their acting as though they were capable of doing that which the British had prohibited them from doing. Now one might argue that the British never really assumed that the Indian population was not equally capable of making salt. This is undoubtedly true. However, the salt laws themselves treated the Indians as less than equal in this regard, and the challenge mounted by the salt marchers was directly to that less-than-equal treatment. In that way, it was akin to the lunch counter sit-ins, where what was at issue was not the ability of the participants to order lunch for themselves, but their equal access to doing so.

Other aspects of the campaign also reflected the presupposition of equality. After the Salt March, there were the attempts to occupy the British salt production facility, the distribution of leaflets and other information, participation in refusal to pay taxes, the local making of salt, and other forms of disobedience and noncooperation. All of these activities were open to anyone who was willing to hew to standards of nonviolence, and it was assumed that anyone could do so.

Moreover, underlying the local goal of removing the onerous salt regulations was the more global goal of ending the British occupation. This goal itself assumes that Indians were perfectly capable of governing themselves, that they were equal to the British in this regard. Moreover, the practices of the protest, involving public participation, coordination of activities, cooperation among protestors, etc. were not only in the service of reaching that goal; they were instantiations of the presupposition of Indians being equally capable of governing themselves. In the term we have seen before, the protests were exercises in *prefiguring* the kind of cooperative governance of which the British assumed they were incapable. To be sure, this prefiguration was not a formal one. Unlike, for instance, the Estonian revolution, the protests did not involve the formation of a parallel government. However, in a less formal way the unfolding of the Salt Satyagraha displayed the kind of social and political cooperation necessary for sustaining a healthy polity. (Unfortunately, of course, later events, especially the rising tensions between Muslims and Hindus, would shatter this cooperation. However, that was of course no proof that the Indian population was less capable of governing itself than the British were capable of governing it.)

So far, we have discussed the role of the presupposition of equality in displaying before the adversary the equality of those who are deemed less than equal. I use the term *displaying before* rather than *displaying to*, because, as Rancière emphasizes, acting on the presupposition of equality is not primarily a matter of demanding recognition from the adversary but instead of acting as an equal. If it were primarily the former, it would still be asking something of the adversary and therefore still be in a position of inequality. To act on the presupposition of equality is to act *as though one were already an equal* rather than *asking to be treated as an equal*. It is the performance of rather than the request for equality. We can see that especially clearly in the lunch counter sit-ins and the Salt Satyagraha.

This does not mean that there are no demands associated with acting under the presupposition of equality, or with nonviolence generally. There are always demands. But there is a difference between demands that come from a position of presupposed inferiority and those that come from a position of presupposed equality. Most nonviolence is structured in accordance with the latter. (We need the term *most* because some activities we have seen as nonviolent, such as writing a letter to a congressperson, need not involve an experienced equality. However, full nonviolent campaigns would not be structured in this way.) What the adversary is confronted with in nonviolence is a group of people (and their supporters) who, in one way or another, have been treated as less than equal but are acting as equals. In so acting, they may even demonstrate a moral superiority – think here of the role moral jiu-jitsu plays in nonviolence. However, even when demonstrating moral superiority, participants in nonviolence are not acting under the presupposition of superiority. That would undermine their position by showing them to be mirror image of those they resist. Rather, their moral superiority lies in acting on the presupposition, as Rancière has it, of the equality of every speaking being.

All of this is in relation to the adversary. As Rancière emphasizes, however, there is another side to this coin. Acting on the presupposition of equality is not only a demonstration *before* the adversary; it is also a demonstration *to* oneself. Rancière writes that acting from the presupposition of equality "is the definition of a struggle for equality which can never be merely a demand upon the other, nor a pressure put upon him, but always simultaneously a proof given to oneself. This is what 'emancipation' means."[20] By invoking the term emancipation, Rancière is turning our attention from the external dynamics of acting under the presupposition of equality to its internal ones in a way that is centrally an aspect of nonviolence that we have not yet discussed.

Gene Sharp notes, in a vein similar to that of Rancière, that nonviolence has important effects on the group itself. He writes that, "the people end their submissiveness and learn a technique of action which shows they are no longer powerless. They are also likely to experience a growth of internal group solidarity. Certain psychological changes will occur which spring from their new sense of power and increase their self-respect. Finally, members of the group which uses nonviolent action seem during and after the struggle to cooperate more on common tasks."[21] It is also a common theme appearing in the work of King and Gandhi. Its importance is not difficult to see. People who are oppressed by others or by a social order often come to despair at their own impotence. They feel like failures, and while resenting the people or social order that oppresses them may even come to identity with the presupposition of inequality – their inequality – operating in it. The personal or structural violence involved may be internalized. After all, it is a short step from continually feeling powerless to feeling inferior. And even where this step is not taken, one can easily come to feel that one is not simply powerless now, but that one will never be able to change one's circumstances.

Many forms of rebellion are refusals of one's powerlessness. Resisting powerlessness is not solely the province of nonviolent resistance. However, the dynamics of nonviolence give a particular cast to that refusal, one that can have a deeper effect on one's sense not only of power but of equality as well. That is what Rancière is seeking to capture with the term *emancipation*. In nonviolence, one does not express one's equality with a gun but rather with one's own body. It is oneself, not one's weapon, which is the vehicle of resistance. This can offer a sense, at once psychological and moral, of one's strength and one's equality to those one opposes. Moreover, in nonviolence it is by standing up rather than knocking down another that expresses refusal. In this way, one asserts one's equality not by lowering the other but by raising oneself – or better, by seeing oneself as larger than one might have otherwise done. To put the point in terms developed by the previous chapter, by displaying dignified behavior one reminds oneself (or convinces oneself) of one's own dignity. That is a form of emancipation that comes not from what is granted by one's adversary but developed through one's own activity.

There is an implication that the respect for dignity and especially the presupposition that equality has for politics is one that cannot be discussed fully here but deserves notice. Rancière claims that if equality is the measure of democracy, then no constitutional order will, ultimately, be democratic. Rather, democracy lies with the people who act on behalf of the presupposition of their equality. Otherwise put, democracy is not a matter of distributive justice; it is a matter of egalitarian action. As Rancière puts the point, "Every politics is democratic in this precise sense: not in the sense of a set of institutions, but in the sense of forms of expression that confront the logic of equality with the logic of the police order."[22] In short, a politics that seeks to ground itself in an ethics akin to the second and third formulations of the categorical imperative as we have modified them, is probably better realized in forms of radical egalitarian action than in a constitutional order. This is a thought that likely did not occur to Kant, and it is not, to my knowledge, a central tenet of current mainstream political philosophy. That neglect, to my mind, has more to do with the trajectory and dominance of the liberal tradition in political philosophy than with the relation of ethics to democracy. However, the central place of ethics in political action is perhaps instantiated in nonviolence more than anywhere else.

Recall that among the three types of violence discussed in the second chapter, the last one is structural. It concerns the ways in which social, political, and economic structures can violate the dignity of an individual. Constitutional orders often do that. Having a constitution was no bar to the treatment of African-Americans in the southern part of the United States. The constitutions of many European countries do not stem the racism – some of it institutionalized – that haunts those countries. Constitutions are not built on the presupposition of equality in the way nonviolent movements are. Because of this, campaigns of nonviolence are more likely not only to oppose structural violence, which is often the goal of such campaigns, but also more likely not to engage in such violence among their participants. This is in contrast to violent campaigns, which because of their military nature, are far more hierarchical.

This does not mean that there are no hierarchies in nonviolent campaigns. In the American Civil Rights movement, for instance, there were often complaints that religious leaders exercised undue influence on the direction of the movement. However, since the character of a nonviolent campaign requires internal as well as external respect for dignity and the presupposition of equality, this is less likely to happen as egregiously as in either a violent campaign or a constitutional order. Again, we must recognize the strength of nonviolence without romanticizing it. And inasmuch as nonviolence does respect dignity and presuppose equality, it fosters a more democratic – if at times more fleeting – political arrangement.

One might want to complain at this point that to view democracy this way is to lose its tie to any political order. Inasmuch as societies are in one way or another bound to constitutional or other legal orders, and there cannot be a truly democratic political order of this type, then we have lost something important in withdrawing the idea of democracy from these orders. If we cannot say of some constitutional or legal orders that they are more democratic than others, then we wind up painting them all with too broad a brushstroke, and failing to distinguish between more and less just orders.

There is something right in this thought, and something wrong as well. There are, of course, better and worse political orders, more and less just *police* orders, to use Rancière's terms. Moreover, there are political orders that are more or less nearly democratic, if we want to use that terminology. Put another way, there are political orders that more or less treat their members as equals. Rancière is quick to concede both that police orders will always be with us, and that we can and should distinguish between the better and worse ones.

However, if we assimilate the idea of democracy to that of political orders that are, ultimately, hierarchical in their character, we risk losing the central idea that has come to be associated with democracy: that of equality. I believe the dominance of neoliberal theory and practice – a central topic of the concluding chapter – is recent evidence of that. It is not that we can do without police orders of one sort or another. Whether we can is a question, at least at this point, of speculation. Moreover, there can be better and worse police orders. None of this, however, should be confused with democracy as the presupposition of the equality of anyone and everyone. This is an idea that we must keep alive, one that we must not dilute in the hierarchies that are our ether.

Rancière insists that, "Democracy first of all means this: anarchic 'government,' one based on nothing other than the absence of every title to govern."[23] This, I have argued, is the thought we should associate with a democratic politics and a thought we should associate with broadly Kantian ethics and ultimately with nonviolence. In a world where many vie for the opportunity to lead us, it offers a way of thinking that allows us to consider the possibility, to one extent or another and in the ways possible, of leading ourselves. It is a framework for bringing a dignity to politics, *our* dignity to politics, instead of allowing it to be the sad and ignoble affair it so often is. It is a framework that allows us to see one another as fellow human beings, worthy not simply of our business but also of our respect. And although, as I have conceded, it may not ultimately supply us with a blueprint for a just social or political order, it has at least the virtue of reminding us of who it is that composes, sustains, and ultimately can challenge any political order, and of the promise of democracy on which such a challenge can be based.

To conclude these two chapters on the values of nonviolence, we should step back and address the general moral character of nonviolence, especially in its comparison with campaigns of violence. One might want to conclude from these reflections that nonviolence is moral while violence is immoral. This would be too hasty and sweeping a claim. It would, in fact, be mistaken on both ends. There is violence that can be moral and nonviolence that can be immoral, on both the individual and collective levels. Turning first to violence, at the individual level very few people would consider violent self-defense to be immoral. To be sure, there are a few pacifists who would deny one the right even to self-defense. But for most of us, if self-defense must be performed violently, this is morally acceptable. This seems to me to be justifiable, even if it involves a denial of the dignity of the attacker. In self-defense, if it is necessary for one's survival, then someone's ability to live a dignified life is going to be at risk, and there is no reason that the one who has not instigated the risk should be able to defend her own. In nonviolence one voluntarily undertakes a risk to oneself, but such a risk is not required of everyone and does not extend to cases where one is involuntarily attacked. Such violence, if justified, has strict moral limits. In most cases, one should not engage in more violence than is necessary to repel an attack. (Although as I write these lines, many states here in the USA have adopted "Stand Your Ground" laws, which allow lethal attacks even when one feels remotely threatened.)

What goes for individuals can go for larger social groups. It may be necessary in some cases to engage in violence against an oppressive adversary. I believe these cases are fewer than are often claimed, but there is no reason to rule them out altogether. The classic example here would be that of the Nazis. Although there were many avenues of nonviolent resistance to their rule – of which the Danish resistance we saw in the previous chapter was one – it is unlikely that without violence the Nazis would have been stopped. Some have argued otherwise. Dustin Howes, for instance, has tried to make the case that a concerted satyagraha against the Nazis might have succeeded. "Only the belief that most German soldiers had a special penchant for inhumanity," he writes, "allows us to think that the German Army would have continued apace with the destruction of Europe if all of Europe and the Russians had refused to destroy them. In combination with the fact that ruling over satyagrahis would be extraordinarily difficult, it seems at least plausible to assume that an Allied force using satyagraha could have bent the will of Germany."[24] Howes imagines that a widespread satyagraha of refusal to cooperate would have made carrying out the Holocaust much more difficult, and notes that the Germans felt the need to hide their intentions because of the opposition revealing them would cause.

This may seem to some, as it does to me, an unlikely scenario, and Howes does not suggest that it is. Moreover, he hedges his argument, not claiming that satyagraha would definitely have worked, especially when it came to the destruction of the Jews. However, even if we grant Howes the argument that a concerted satyagraha might have worked, we needn't conclude that violent resistance against the Nazis was immoral. The case would be analogous with that of individual self-defense. There may be, in such cases, avenues of escape that would not involve violence against the adversary and that *might* work. However, one is not required to abandon violent self-defense and resort to them on the basis of this possibility. Moreover, in collective cases there is an even weaker moral pull, since success hangs not only upon what one does but in addition on the cooperation of everyone else.

If violence is not necessarily immoral, neither is nonviolence necessarily moral. One can use nonviolent means toward immoral ends, although examples here would be rarer. One of the reasons for this is that what might look like nonviolent actions could in fact turn out to be violent. For instance, I believe that what are called nonviolent demonstrations against and blockades of abortion clinics are immoral. However, the reason for this is that denying a woman the ability to end an unwanted pregnancy is a violation of her dignity in the precise sense discussed in the second chapter. There is very little more central in constructing a life for oneself than the decision whether to bear and raise a child. Therefore, it seems to me that, surface appearances aside, many aspects of the anti-abortion movement are in fact violent.

This analysis would apply to many cases where nonviolent resistance is directed against those whose dignity is at stake, making the examples of immoral nonviolence more difficult to conceive. Such a case would have to involve nonviolent resistance against something that was immoral to resist but not an instance of something that violated dignity. Imagine, for instance, that a nonviolent demonstration blockaded the headquarters of a newspaper that had printed a controversial article. The demonstration was not intended to close the newspaper permanently, but simply to try to persuade the editors not to print such articles. Such a demonstration might be considered immoral – since it was seeking to undermine freedom of the press – without rising to the level of violence.

However, if violence can be moral and nonviolence immoral, is there no moral difference between the two? This chapter and the last one show otherwise. While we cannot make sweeping claims about the necessary superiority of nonviolence, we can say that nonviolence is morally superior to violence in respecting two related values: dignity and equality. Whereas violent campaigns, perhaps of necessity, violate the dignity of the adversary and the presupposition of equality, nonviolent campaigns do not (or at least do not to a far greater extent). While this does not make a decisive case for nonviolence over violence in all situations, it privileges nonviolence as the moral default in cases of resistance. In other words, where resistance against oppression or other social ills has become necessary, nonviolence should be considered the most appropriate response, barring special justification for violence. If violence is proposed as a better response than nonviolence, the case should be made for it. Failing that, nonviolence should prevail as the morally required course of action.

6
Nonviolence in Today's World

Over the course of this book, we have isolated nonviolence as a particular way to conduct political, social, and/or economic resistance. It seeks to change arrangements that are considered by its participants – and often by nonparticipants – as unjust, oppressive, unfair, or deleterious. In this, nonviolence is like other forms of resistance, particularly violent ones. What distinguishes nonviolence from violent forms of political change does not lie necessarily in its ultimate goals, but in its means. This is why nonviolence can be pragmatic and not just principled. However, means are often inseparable from the ends they promote. As a result, the means employed by nonviolent campaigns often result in different – and, as we have seen, more successfully attained – ends than those of violent campaigns.

What characterizes nonviolence can at first be approached negatively. Nonviolence abjures violence, and in particular certain kinds of violence. It abjures the violence that denigrates the dignity of others, whether that violence is physical, psychological, or structural. That dignity, in turn, is founded in the ability of others, including one's adversary, to conduct a human life, a life of meaningful projects free from threat of death or imposed impoverishment. However, the negative approach to nonviolence, when adequately described, yields a more positive view. Nonviolence is characterized by the presence of at least two fundamental values: dignity and equality. In nonviolence everyone – participants, adversaries, and bystanders – is considered to possess dignity, and because of this is to be approached in a dignified manner, where the latter is a matter of preserving dignity in the former sense. Moreover, and related, everyone is considered to be equally capable of conceiving and conducting a human life alongside others.

These values, of course, while respected behaviorally, are not required as a matter of belief among the participants in nonviolent struggle. Those who embrace nonviolence simply as a more practical form of resistance may not believe in the dignity and equality of their adversaries. They might, if it were feasible, prefer to do violence to those against whom their campaigns are directed. However, as long as those campaigns are conducted in accordance with the norms dictated by nonviolence, the dignity and equality of adversaries will be preserved, in fact if not in desire.

Nonviolence, whether pragmatic or principled, will, because of its normative commitments, issue out into particular dynamics of struggle. The most striking of these is moral or at least political jiu-jitsu. In certain nonviolent struggles, the oppression of the adversary reacts back against him or her or them, making others and then themselves consider their position in a different moral light from the one they had previously seen themselves under. Moral jiu-jitsu turns the ethical tables on an adversary, so that what had once appeared as justified actions or policies turns out to be an unjustified assault upon the dignity of those who resist them. Moral jiu-jitsu is in one sense the purist of nonviolent dynamics, since it results in a convergence on a common moral view that includes protestors and adversaries on the same moral plane.

However, nonviolent dynamics are not restricted to that of moral jiu-jitsu. There are dynamics of accommodation and even of coercion. It is possible to force an adversary into a course of action, one that is taken up involuntarily, without violating dignity or presupposing inequality. This can happen through political jiu-jitsu, but is not restricted to it. The refusal of obedience to and even the active disruption of an unjust political, economic, or social order can be done while preserving the norms of nonviolence. Nonviolence is not acquiescence; nor is it exhausted by a fruitless appeal to the conscience of the other. As long as it retains behavioral (if not psychologically committed) respect for the dignity of the other, it is compatible with a variety of coercive tactics, from simple refusal to participate to public demonstrations to forming human barriers.

There is often a tendency to think of nonviolence as either a naive approach to politics, or one that may have had relevance at one time but is now passé. The former view generally relies on an overly simplistic conception of nonviolence as either simply persuasion or at most moral jiu-jitsu. While it is true that many adversaries are, given their positions of power and privilege, unlikely to be persuaded to abandon those positions, and while it is true that moral jiu-jitsu often fails to materialize, it is false to conclude from these that nonviolence requires an unrealistic view of human nature. As we have seen, many struggles are at once nonviolent and coercive, taking full measure of the oppressive character of their adversaries. The latter view – of nonviolence as passé – is often based on seeing nonviolence through a particular historical lens: that of the struggles of Indian Independence and the American Civil Rights movements. Through the lens of history, Gandhi and King are seen as towering figures that, during a certain historical period, were able to engage in romantic struggles that are no longer available to us.

This impression is belied by the recent and diverse examples of nonviolence that have occurred in the world. Consider, for instance, the examples we canvassed at the outset of the book. The oldest one, that of the Philippines, is from the mid-1980s. The Estonian Revolution took place over the late 1980s and early 1990s, and Tahrir Square and Occupy only several years ago. Currently (early 2014), there are other nonviolent movements alive throughout the world. In Brazil, the MST (*Movimento dos Trabalhadores Sem Terra*) is a movement of peasants seeking to occupy and produce on land owned by large agricultural corporations. Although the movement has been periodically engaged in destruction of property, it is unclear that this destruction meets the criteria for violence laid out in the second chapter of this book. Usually, destroyed property includes equipment used by agribusiness that replaces the need for peasant labor. Destroying it does not violate the dignity of the owners. And elsewhere, for instance in the Palestinian-occupied territories, there have been a number of nonviolent resistance actions, from protests against the building of the "apartheid" wall separating areas of Palestine from Israel – and from one another – to the BDS (Boycott, Divestment, Sanctions) Movement seeking to isolate Israel in much the same way South Africa was isolated in the 1980s.

Contemporary nonviolent movements are not backward-looking campaigns based on nostalgia. While they are often aware of the history and dynamics of nonviolence, the most creative among them seek to employ tactics that are responsive to the contexts in which they arise and to which they must respond. Moreover, not only are there examples of nonviolence, there is also a need for it. In much of the world, the existence of occupations, dictatorship, exploitation, and structural violence calls out for redress. And as we have seen from Chenoweth and Stephan's work, in the areas of anti-regime and anti-occupation movements, the historical record of nonviolent movements is far more promising than that of violent ones. As I write, the Egyptian situation, so promising after the events of Tahrir Square and across Egypt, seems to be devolving into a military dictatorship that is betraying the goals of the Arab Spring. There are those, of course, who will argue that it was the military all along who used the protests in order to gain power. However, even if one grants this, just as it would have been more difficult to gain power without riding on the back of the largely nonviolent movement in Egypt, so it would be difficult for the military to sustain power in the face of massive nonviolent refusal to obey. There are certainly sparks of disobedience, and much discontent, arising in Egypt at this moment.

However, if we turn our attention from situations of obvious oppression and exploitation to more subtle ones, we may find a greater difficulty in understanding the role of nonviolence. Confronting a dictatorship or an occupation or obviously discriminatory laws or massive agricultural property concentration is one thing; confronting an economic order that is more subtly exploitative is another. In the former cases, the adversary is often easy to identify. It is the dictator or the occupiers or the discriminatory politician or populace or the landowner who is to be resisted. In the latter case, the adversaries are more diverse and more difficult to identify. And among the adversaries can be the system itself. Just as recognizing physical and psychological violence is easier than recognizing structural violence, so understanding and confronting the exploitative economic order of the day is more difficult than traditional campaigns struggling against political oppression or obvious economic inequities. This was something that Martin Luther King discovered when he turned his attention from traditional racial discrimination to economic inequality. It has been rediscovered by the alter-globalization movement that protested in Seattle and elsewhere and more recently by Occupy, both of which sought to call attention to the massive inequities of wealth and resources that characterize the current economic order.

We cannot, of course, come to terms with the economic shape of our world in the short conclusion to this book. However, it would be worth pausing a moment over some of the changes that have taken place in the USA and Europe over the past several decades, and to ask what role nonviolence might have in confronting those changes. Of course, what happens economically in the USA and Europe has profound effects elsewhere, but we can see it more clearly if we focus our attention more narrowly on those areas. What we see if we look there is a decline of the welfare state that held sway in the period between the Great Depression and the early 1980s, and a turn to what has often come to be called *neoliberalism*.[1]

Neoliberalism refers to an economic order whose beginnings are associated with the administrations of Ronald Reagan in the USA and Margaret Thatcher in the UK. Its major intellectual center is the economics department at the University of Chicago. In fact, neoliberalism is often called Chicago School economics. One way to approach it would be through a contrast with the Keynesian economics that dominated the Depression and post-Depression era.

Keynes' work became dominant during the Depression as a response to the more laissez-faire economics previous to his own writing. In his major work, *A General Theory of Employment, Interest, and Money*, Keynes challenges the laissez-faire orthodoxy by arguing that markets are not necessarily self-correcting, and under certain circumstances require government intervention in order for them to flourish. More specifically, the government needs to stimulate demand in order for economies to recover, particularly when the interest rate is low and business investment is not forthcoming. In order to stimulate demand, Keynes recommended governmental deficit spending in the form of public investment. Adopting the Keynesian view led the US government under Franklin Roosevelt to create a massive program of public works across the country, and helped initiate such programs as Social Security. After World War II, the Keynesian program justified government intervention into the economy through various public welfare measures as well as government stimulation efforts. During this period, however, the Chicago School was arguing for less government intervention into the economy.

Their rise was abetted in the early 1970s by the Arab Oil Embargo and the subsequent "stagflation" in the USA and elsewhere. Stagflation is a combination of inflation and economic stagnation, a combination that seemed to contradict Keynes' view. For him, inflation would be a sign that demand was high, so it would seem to coincide with economic activity rather than stagnation. The degree to which stagflation provides a refutation of Keynes' thought is a controversial one, but with the election of Thatcher in 1979 and Reagan in 1980, the moment for the Chicago School had come, and it remains with us, even though many would argue – myself included – that the Great Recession of 2008 should have laid neoliberalism to rest.

What is neoliberalism? The political thinker David Harvey defines it as, "a theory of political economic practices that proposes that human wellbeing can best be advanced by liberating individual entrepreneurial freedoms and skills within an institutional framework characterized by strong private property rights, free markets, and free trade."[2] Neoliberalism involves a particular set of interventions into various national markets. In particular, supported by the World Bank and especially the International Monetary Fund, it has sought to promote deregulation, privatization, and the withdrawal of the public sector from social services. (More recently, there has been a slight softening of this position in World Bank and IMF quarters.) We have seen this program at work in the

USA, and it remains the framework for much public policy in the USA and Europe. Deregulation is the removing of government oversight in various areas of the economy. For instance, in the USA it involved the removal of restrictions on commercial banks in regard to financial investment, as well as allowing the creation of various esoteric derivatives that were at the center of the 2008 economic meltdown. Privatization is the selling of government-owned productive operations to private businesses, such as the 1993 privatization of the British railway system. The withdrawal of the public sector from social services occurs when the government stops engaging in public welfare activities, such as President Bill Clinton's cutbacks on welfare during the 1990s or the cutbacks to university education that are happening across the UK and, at the moment to a lesser extent, in the USA.

Although the brief examples in the previous paragraph refer to the two most enthusiastic supporters of neoliberalism, it has been more or less adopted in large parts of Europe. As important, it has been forced upon many poorer countries that find themselves in debt, in what was once known as "structural adjustment." These policies, adopted by the International Monetary Fund and, to a lesser extent, the World Bank, required privatization, deregulation, and cutbacks in social services as a condition of monetary investment, often resulting in the further impoverishment of already struggling populations.

For Harvey, neoliberalism has been a tactic of class struggle, an attempt by the wealthier classes to shift wealth back in their direction. He sees neoliberalism "as a *political* project to re-establish the conditions for capital accumulation and to restore the power of economic elites."[3] In the USA, the massive inequality of the past thirty or forty years has been a topic of public discussion, one that has been highlighted by the Occupy movement. Whether or not neoliberalism is a conscious political project, it has certainly had the effect of concentrating wealth and removing many of the supports characteristic of the Keynesian welfare state.

In addition to economic concentration and consequently greater inequality, it is not difficult to imagine other effects of neoliberalism. We in the USA and the UK – and increasingly in other European countries – live in societies which are far more individualistic than they were under a Keynesian economic order. The reason for this is not far to seek. Where once it was considered an important social duty to assist one's fellow citizens, now they are left more nearly to their own devices. With the decline in support for public assistance, higher education, union solidarity, and even backing for the arts, people are left to rely on their own resources in order to gain many of the social goods supposedly available in a polity. This affects not only those who are currently struggling; it has an impact on the rest of us as well. After all, there are very few of us who are more than a layoff away from relying on public support. And with the decline of corporate loyalty toward long-term workers, that prospect is never very far from awareness. (In fact, as a tenured professor, I have one of the few secure jobs left in the neoliberal economy. And universities, under financial duress, are doing what they can to hire professors off the tenure track.)

When people know they are bereft of public support if they stumble, they are more likely to act out of fear rather than duress. One must protect what one has, and in doing so use one's resources for one's own protection rather than for a contribution to others in society. This fear, in turn, erodes social solidarity; it contributes to an increasing individualization. People husband their means, seeing others as competitors for those means rather than as fellows in a joint venture of community building. Of course, individualism – particularly in the USA – has been a theme that is coextensive with the country's history. However, under neoliberalism it begins to crowd out other themes that have existed alongside it, such as generosity and optimism.

All of this has two related effects: it reproduces the neoliberal economic order and it blunts the project of resistance to it. The dynamic of reproduction is this: When one removes support for individuals through privatization, deregulation, and withdrawal of public services, people are left, as we have just seen, to fend for themselves. In trying to make the most of their resources, they will be loathe to part with them for the larger social good, thus reinforcing the withdrawal of public services. In addition, people will begin to distrust governmental action, which requires taxation – governments run on taxes. This leads both to privatization and deregulation, since both are products of the distrust of governments. Privatization is a response to the idea that governments handle people's money inefficiently, which in turn comes from the fear that, as Ronald Reagan put it, "Government is not the solution; it is the problem." Deregulation allows companies to act on their own recognizance, which allows them to generate greater profits without governmental oversight, and which in turn comes to be seen as economically imperative in a precarious economic environment. Thus neoliberalism leads to more neoliberalism in a cycle of isolated individualism creating more isolated individualism.

The erosion of social solidarity thus created blunts the ability of people to resist the neoliberal order. By isolating individuals from one another, it becomes difficult to instill the kind of cooperative spirit necessary for successful social movements. If others are simply rivals for scarce resources or wealth, then it is difficult to see how a movement of social resistance can arise. Social resistance requires a social orientation, which itself must be had on the basis of a kind of trust of or empathy for the other that is marginalized by the competitive individualism promoted by the neoliberal order. There has, of course, been much discussion about the decline of the left in industrialized countries. I believe that we can find part of the cause for this in the way neoliberalism reproduces itself through the kinds of self-centeredness it creates.

Another part of the difficulty of resistance lies in the diffuse character of what I have been describing here. Neoliberalism is an economic order that is not the product of particular individuals seeking to concentrate wealth while fooling everyone else into being competitors – or at least not largely that. Unlike the object of previous nonviolent campaigns, it is difficult to sort out whom exactly to confront and what to confront them about. Neoliberalism has no Marcoses or Mubaraks. It has no occupying Soviet Union. What it does have, and what the Occupy movement sought to confront, is a diffuse but small set of winners and a much larger and more diffuse set of losers (or at least stagnators) who emerge out of an inegalitarian mode of economic operation. Confronting an economic order is far more difficult than confronting a person, a regime, or a law or set of laws. The change required is more global, particularly since, in the case of neoliberalism, companies operate transnationally as well as nationally.

There are, then, at least two challenges presented by neoliberalism: the undermining of solidarity through a rampant individualism and the difficulty of finding targets or objects for political resistance. Regarding the first, nonviolence can certainly provide a countervailing force. This is because the normative commitments of nonviolence run directly counter to those of neoliberalism. While neoliberalism promotes competition, distrust, and isolation, nonviolence promotes cooperation, trust, and solidarity. The values infusing nonviolence – dignity and equality – require seeing our fellow human beings (and often other animals) precisely as fellows, worthy of our recognition and respect. Even where there is conflict – and why would there be nonviolence if there were no conflict? – this conflict is limited, at least on one side, by the boundaries the core values of nonviolence places upon its actors.

One might object here that in reality nonviolence is characterized precisely by competition, a competition between those who engage in it and their adversary. This is a conflict of visions in which one must prevail at the expense of the other. What, then, it might be asked, is the difference between this type of competition and the market competition promoted under neoliberalism?

There certainly can be a kind of competitive aspect characteristic of nonviolence. This would show up not so much in cases of moral jiu-jitsu but in cases of nonviolent coercion, where each side presses against the other and only one can succeed. However, even in cases like this, the competition characteristic of nonviolence is very different from that characteristic of neoliberalism. We might say that in nonviolence what is at stake is a conflict of visions in which one vision – that of nonviolence – is inextricable from the preservation of the dignity of individuals. That is to say, nonviolence, even where it is not principled but only pragmatic, treats others (as Kant would have it) as ends rather than simply as means. The other is not there merely to benefit oneself but must be taken to have an independent life worthy of behavioral if not psychological respect.

This is not true of neoliberalism. The naked competition promoted by a neoliberal order submits everything to a market bereft of a moral framework. Where community solidarity is undermined in favor of individual competition, there is no motivation to treat others as anything more than means to one's ends. The privatization, deregulation, and withdrawal from social services that are the pillars of the neoliberal order are invitations to self-aggrandizement at the expense of fellowship. This invitation is augmented by the fear we discussed above. Where social solidarity is lacking, others can only be seen as competitors for the same set of scarce goods without which one is left without resources to support oneself or one's family. Although both neoliberalism and nonviolence can be characterized in terms of competition, then, their competitive natures emerge out of very different views of what it is for human beings to be with one another.

If the values of nonviolence cut against those of neoliberalism and can therefore provide an alternative to it, how about the second issue we have raised, that of targets or objects? Resisting neoliberalism is more difficult than resisting an unjust political order. Its operations are more elusive, the structural violence it promotes more subtle than the overt violence characteristic of a tyrannical political regime or an occupation or a structure of racist segregation. How might nonviolence operate in an environment where the problem is not the actions of individuals or laws but the economic system itself?

To be sure, there has been resistance to the neoliberal economic order, and much of it has been nonviolent. What was sometimes called the anti-globalization movement, but is properly better named the alter-globalization movement, was directed at institutions that support neoliberalism at the international level: the World Trade Organization, the International Monetary Fund, and the World Bank, among others. The most well-known demonstration took place in late November, 1999 in Seattle, drawing tens of thousands of people and succeeding in forcing the cancellation of the opening ceremonies of the World Trade Organization meeting that year. Although there was violence at that demonstration – which lasted the four days of the WTO meetings – much of it was in response to police brutality. More important, the bulk of the demonstrations was, in fact, nonviolent.

There are other campaigns that have sought to challenge neoliberalism as well, violent as well as nonviolent. In the case of the former, the Zapatistas in Mexico, working on behalf and alongside of the indigenous people of Chiapas, saw the problems of the indigenous as inseparable from neoliberalism, which they labeled as such.[4] Among the former, we should certainly count Occupy (although there were moments of violence, for example in Oakland Occupy). Occupy might be seen as the inheritor of the alter-globalization movement. Although it focused on the concentration of wealth in the USA, its economic concerns intersect with those of the alter-globalization movement, for whom economic inequality was a central target. Moreover, there is a cycle of mutual reinforcement between neoliberalism and the concentration of wealth. Deregulation, privatization, and the withdrawal from public services concentrates wealth at the top. That concentration, in turn, allows wealth-owners to promote more deregulation, privatization, and further cuts to social services. So by focusing on the one percent, Occupy directly addresses one of the central aspects of neoliberalism.

Another movement that challenges the concentration of wealth is one that we mentioned briefly above: the *Movimento dos Trabalhadores Sem Terra*, or MST. Its struggles for land for peasants to work is a direct challenge to the concentration of wealth that is also Occupy's concern. In addition, in Argentina, the movement of worker takeover of factories that started in the Argentian economic meltdown of 2001 has provided another model of resistance to economic concentration.[5] Argentinian workers have taken over abandoned factories in much the same way that peasants have taken over unused land in Brazil, and have done so in response to overtly neoliberal policies adopted in Argentina over the decade previous to that country's crisis. Both movements constitute largely nonviolent challenges to the concentration of wealth that is protected in the name of private property, a concentration itself that is either the result of or exacerbated by neoliberal policies.

All three cases – Occupy, MST, and the Argentinian factory takeovers – have been characterized by occupation: of either public or privately owned spaces, of agricultural land, and of factories. Of course, the latter two occupations have been different from those of Occupy, since they involve the seizure of productive resources in order to make a living. However, there may be something to the fact of occupation, as opposed to traditional demonstration, that poses a particular challenge to neoliberalism. Traditional demonstrations take place in designated public areas and are time-limited. Occupations are more temporally open-ended and often involve spaces that are not considered publicly available. There are two results of this. First, occupations challenge the privatization of particular spaces, and through that can challenge neoliberal concentrations of wealth. Second, occupying privately owned spaces, or staying in public ones indefinitely, are more likely to provoke challenges among authorities, which in turn make it more likely that the associated campaigns will receive public attention. It may be, then, that different forms of occupation become tactics in nonviolent campaigns to challenge neoliberalism.

However these challenges arise, their common difficulty is that of finding points of resistance to an oppression that is more economic than political. While, as we have seen, there are in our world plenty of traditional political oppressions that cry out for nonviolent resistance, the oppression – indeed the structural violence – associated with neoliberal global capitalism and its concentrations of wealth, decline of public services, and isolation of individuals, presents a unique set of problems for nonviolent (and indeed for any) resistance. The MST and Argentinian factory takeover movement have succeeded in finding apt places of intervention, allowing them to reclaim their work as a form of economic resistance. With Occupy, matters are more difficult, since their challenge is more globally to an economic system than more locally to one of its particular effects. Perhaps, however, through the linkages between various struggles, both local and global, a revived alter-globalization movement can arise, one that calls attention to specific symptoms of neoliberalism and at the same time to the economic order that creates those symptoms.

Such a movement will have to be, for pragmatic if not principled reasons, largely nonviolent. There are several reasons for this. First, the target or targets of campaigns against neoliberalism and its effects are often institutions and practices rather than individuals, and the violence neoliberalism creates is generally more structural than physical or psychological. It is in the way of going about economic activity and the effects upon us that neoliberalism has that must be opposed. It is impossible to oppose practices with violence, because practices only exist in their instantiation by people's behavior, and many of the people who instantiate neoliberalism are its victims rather than its beneficiaries. And even those who are its beneficiaries are often more a product of neoliberalism than its producer. Attacking such institutions and practices will involve a lot of widespread education about how we think about our world as well as creative nonviolent ways of demonstrating its effects. Occupy, the MST, and the Argentian factory takeovers are steps in that direction, and perhaps provide lessons in how to proceed.

Second, even inasmuch as there are particular individuals who wield the power that supports neoliberalism, they are usually unarmed. They are bankers, financiers, officials in institutions like the World Bank and the International Monetary Fund, and national political figures. Attacking these people violently will result in a jiu-jitsu that rebounds against those who engage in it. Although there may be no moral jiu-jitsu – those who attack these unarmed supporters of neoliberalism may not become convinced that they were mistaken in their goals – they will fail to gain public sympathy for their campaigns. The sympathy will go to the other side. Moreover, unlike the case with some of the more overtly egregious dictatorships and occupations, those who run the institutions that support neoliberalism are often as taken in by it as everyone else. Most of them likely believe sincerely that they are engaged in an activity that benefits their communities and their world. In this, they are perhaps more like many average Southern whites during segregation in the USA than they are like Mubarak or the Soviet authorities in Estonia. (One might argue here that the latter were as self-deceived about their roles as the Southern whites were. Such a discussion would take things far afield into the question of the character and extent of self-deception. I might only note here that, even if they were self-deceived – a position with which I have some sympathy – the evidence of their egregiousness was more readily available to them than it was to average [as opposed to elite] Southern whites, if only because of the insularity of the South during the period of Jim Crow.)

Finally, although those who uphold neoliberalism are usually unarmed, the neoliberal order is backed up by overwhelming military and police support. If unarmed politicians and economic actors are the hinges upon which neoliberalism turns, the military institutions of many of the world's most technologically advanced countries will seek to ensure that those hinges are not undone. Matching the potential violence of these institutions is an impossible task. So, for reasons that are purely pragmatic, in the struggle against neoliberalism the attempt to enact a violent overthrow of neoliberal institutions will be a quixotic one. It will be quickly suppressed.

For all these reasons, the struggle against the neoliberal order, if it is to succeed, must be a nonviolent one. If we combine this conclusion with the recognition that there are also many remaining traditional oppressions that could be challenged by nonviolent resistance, and also with the findings of researchers like Chenoweth and Stephan that nonviolence is generally more successful than violence, then we can recognize the need to think about and act upon nonviolent strategies in our world. Rather than asking how we might *overthrow* the many onerous institutions and practices that surround and indeed pervade our lives, we might instead ask how to *undermine* them. We might ask how to foster a refusal of obedience to them, one that is based upon a recognition of the dignity and a presupposition of the equality of everyone. Rather than repeating the failures of the previous century that attended so many of the violent revolutions that were engaged in, we might look instead to the more successful history of nonviolent struggle. And we might do this not in order to romanticize a lost and glorious past characterized by outsized figures like Gandhi and King, but instead to ask ourselves how to develop the lessons of that past into a future that sorely needs it.

Notes

Chapter 1

1 Much of this account is taken from the extraordinary 2006 film *The Singing Revolution*, directed by James and Maureen Tusty, along with the accompanying book by Priit Vesilind of the same name (Tallinn: Varrak, 2008). For a more extended history of Estonia, see Toivo Raun's *Estonia and the Estonians* (Hoover Institution Press, 2nd edn 2002). I also want to thank Tarmo Jüristo for helpful comments on an earlier draft of this section.

2 Vesilind, *The Singing Revolution*, pp. 125, 129.

3 Tarmo Jüristo, in communication.

4 The events recounted here are drawn from several histories. The magisterial history of twentieth-century nonviolence, Peter Ackerman and Jack DuVall's *A Force More Powerful: A Century of Nonviolent Conflict* (New York: St Martin's Press, 2000), Kurt Schock's *Unarmed Insurrections: People Power Movements in Nondemocracies* (Minneapolis: University of Minnesota Press, 2005), and Erica Chenoweth and Maria J. Stephan's *Why Civil Resistance Works: The Strategic Logic of Nonviolent Conflict* (New York: Columbia University Press, 2011). We will have occasion to return to all of these works, the latter two especially in discussion of the dynamics of nonviolence.

5 Ackerman and DuVall, *A Force More Powerful*, p. 375.

6 Schock, *Unarmed Insurrections*, pp. 75–6.
7 Ackerman and DuVall, *A Force More Powerful*, p. 384.
8 Quoted in Ackerman and DuVall, *A Force More Powerful*, p. 388. The original source is Isabel T. Crisosotomo, *Cory, Profile of a President* (Boston: Branden Publishing Co., 1987), pp. 209–10.
9 This account of the events in Tahrir Square is drawn largely from Hamid Dabashi's *The Arab Spring: The End of Postcolonialism* (London: Zed, 2012); James Gelvin's *The Arab Uprisings: What Everyone Needs to Know* (Oxford: Oxford University Press, 2012); and Lin Noueihed and Alex Warren's *The Battle for the Arab Spring: Revolution, Counter-Revolution, and the Making of a New Era* (New Haven: Yale University Press, 2012). I would also like to thank Dalia Mostafa for her generous reading of and suggestions for an earlier draft of this section.
10 Cited in Gelvin, *The Arab Uprisings*, p. 45.
11 Noueihed and Warren, *The Battle for the Arab Spring*, p. 101.
12 Cited in Gelvin, *The Arab Uprisings*, p. 47.
13 Dabashi, *The Arab Spring*, p. 10.
14 Noueihed and Warren, *The Battle for the Arab Spring*, p. 99.
15 For an informal statistical overview of New York Occupy, see Christine Schweidler, Pablo Rey Mazón, Saba Waheed, and Sasha Constanza-Chock, "Research by and for the Movement: Key findings from the Occupy Research Demographic and Participation Survey," in Khatib, Kate; Killjoy, Margaret; and McGuire, Mike, *We are Many: Reflections on Movement Strategy from Occupation to Liberation*, Oakland: AK Press, 2012, pp. 69–73.
16 There are many informal histories of the Occupy movement, especially New York Occupy. For a short chronology, the Wikipedia page is helpful: http://en.wikipedia.org/wiki/Occupy_Wall_Street. Todd Gitlin's *Occupy Nation: The Roots, the Spirit, and the Promise of Occupy Wall Street* (New York: HarperCollins, 2012), with interviews and thoughtful reflections by Gitlin, is invaluable. A thoughtful, if more theoretical, overview from three perspectives appears in W. J. T. Mitchell, Bernard

Harcourt, and Michael Taussig, *Occupy: Three Inquiries in Disobedience* (Chicago: University of Chicago Press, 2013).

17 For the full document, see pp. 148–9 in *We Are Many*. It is also available online at several places, including the General Assembly's website: http://www.nycga.net/resources/documents/declaration/.

18 See, e.g., Andy Ostroy's "The Occupy Wall Street Movement Needs a Clear Set of Demands," in *The Huffington Post*, http://www.huffingtonpost.com/andy-ostroy/occupy-wall-street-demands_b_999658.html

19 For a good discussion of this contrast by an observer at the time, see Betsy Reed's "Why So Many Demands for Demands?" in *The Nation*, http://www.thenation.com/blog/163762/occupy-wall-street-why-so-many-demands-demands#

20 Gitlin, *Occupy Nation*, p. 73.

21 Ibid., pp. 73–4.

22 For an excellent discussion of this issue, see Mark Lance's "Fetishizing Process," published in 2005 by the Institute for Anarchist Studies, http://www.academia.edu/1110507/fetishizing_process

23 Holmes, Martha, "The Center Cannot Hold: A Revolution in Process," in *We Are Many*, p. 155. Her article describes the various experiments that were made to modify the process while not closing off participation.

24 Gitlin, *Occupy Nation*, pp. 114–15.

25 For a timeline of the events around Occupy New York, see http://en.wikipedia.org/wiki/Timeline_of_Occupy_Wall_Street#November_2011

26 There are numerous accounts of the Salt March, including a short one by Ackerman and DuVall, *A Force More Powerful*, on pp. 85–7.

27 There are several comprehensive histories of the Civil Rights Movement, among them Taylor Branch's *Parting the Waters: America in the King Years, 1954–63* (New York: Simon and Schuster, 1988).

28 This does not mean, of course, that we actually treat our soldiers well or work to keep them safe. For more on this, see Andrew Bacevich's *Breach of Trust: How American Failed Their Soldiers And Their Country* (New York: Metropolitan Books, 2013).

Chapter 2

1 See, for instance, Mark Kurlansky's *Nonviolence: The History of a Dangerous Idea* (New York: Modern Library, 2006), Adam Roberts' and Timothy Garton Ash's edited collection *Civil Resistance and Power Politics: The Experience of Non-Violent Action from Gandhi to the Present* (Oxford: Oxford University Press, 2011) and, from a few years earlier, Peter Ackerman and Jack Duvall's *A Force More Powerful: A Century of Nonviolent Conflict* (New York: St Martin's Press, 2000).

2 For instance, Kurt Schock has studied the success and failure of nonviolent movements in nondemocratic societies in *Unarmed Insurrections: People Power Movements in Nondemocracies* (Minneapolis: University of Minnesota Press, 2005) and Erica Chenoweth and Maria J. Stephan have compared violent and nonviolent insurrections in *Why Civil Resistance Works: The Strategic Logic of Nonviolent Conflict* (New York: Columbia University Press, 2011). We will have occasion to refer to these works in the following chapter.

3 There have been related philosophical reflections such as Kimberley Brownlee's *Conscience and Conviction: The Case for Civil Disobedience* (Oxford: Oxford University Press, 2012). In addition, a collection of Robert Holmes' writings on nonviolence has recently appeared: *The Ethics of Nonviolence: Essays by Robert L. Holmes*, Bloomsbury Press, 2013. This is a collection rather than an extended work, and most of the essays deals with how to live nonviolently rather than the character of nonviolent resistance.

4 The classic systematic statement of nonviolent resistance from the Gandhian tradition remains Joan Bondurant's *The Conquest of Violence: The Gandhian Philosophy of Conflict*, originally published in 1957 (2nd edn, Princeton: Princeton University Press, 1988).

5 This is not to say that nonviolence does not involve undergoing. As Bondurant explains, willingness to suffer is one of the cornerstones of Gandhian nonviolence or satyagraha.

6 King, *Why We Can't Wait*, p. 36.

7 Žižek, Slavoj, *Violence: Six Sideways Reflections* (New York: Picador, 2008), p. 2. Although Žižek does not cite

the literature on this, the original treatment of what was called structural violence is John Galtung's "Violence, Peace, and Peace Research," *Journal of Peace Research*, Vol. 6, no. 3, 1969, pp. 167–91. A discussion of his article appears below.

8 Žižek, *Violence*, p. 61.

9 Audi, Robert, "On the Meaning and Justification of Violence," in *Violence: A Philosophical Anthology*, p. 143.

10 Ibid., p. 147.

11 See note 6, above.

12 Galtung, "Violence, Peace, and Peace Research," p. 168 (italics in original).

13 Ibid., p. 168.

14 Ibid., p. 170.

15 Ibid., p. 171. Galtung recognizes that he is stretching the concept of violence, and at one point says that, "In order not to overwork the word violence we shall sometimes refer to the condition of structural violence as *social injustice*" (p. 171).

16 Coady, C. A. J., "The Idea of Violence," *Journal of Applied Philosophy*, Vol. 3, no. 1, 1986, pp. 3–19.

17 Coady, "The Idea of Violence," p. 7.

18 Ibid., p. 11.

19 He also argues against another definition of violence, which he calls "legitimist" violence, which "incorporates a reference to an illegal or illegitimate use of force." (p. 4) I find his arguments against this view compelling, and so will not discuss it further here.

20 Coady, "The Idea of Violence," p. 4.

21 Ibid., p. 16, quoting from Garver, Newton, "What Violence Is," *The Nation*, Vol. 209, June 24, 1968.

22 Coady, "The Idea of Violence," pp. 15–16.

23 Ibid., p. 16.

24 Ibid., p. 16.

25 Ibid., p. 16, emphasis added.

26 Garver, Newton. "What Violence Is," in *Violence: A Philosophical Anthology*, p. 176.

27 From a more political angle, in her essay *On Violence*, Hannah Arendt also assumes that violence is intentional. In particular, it is intended as a means to achieve certain ends in situations in which other means fail to do so. Cf., esp. *On Violence* (New York: Harcourt, Brace, and World, Inc., 1970), pp. 46–54.

28 Bufacchi, Vittorio, *Violence and Social Justice*, New York: Palgrave Macmillan, 2007, pp. 43–4.

29 Bufacchi, *Violence and Social Justice*, p. 40.

30 MacCallum, Gerald C., "What is Wrong with Violence," in Bufacchi, *Violence: A Philosophical Anthology*, p. 126.

31 I am grateful to Candice Delmas for this example, with which she confronted an earlier attempt of mine to offer a general definition of violence.

32 Bufacchi, *Violence and Social Justice*, pp. 58–9.

33 The confusion of coercion with violence is displayed in Allan Bäck's "Thinking Clearly About Violence," *Philosophical Studies*, Vol. 117, no. 1/2, January 2004, pp. 219–30. This leads him to the untenable conclusion that "Are all types of passive resistance, all strategies of nonviolence violent in the basic sense and hence *prima facie* wrong? Yes." (p. 227) One would think this conclusion to be a *reductio* of the argument for it; however Bäck defends his view against this very possibility by mischaracterizing a passage in Gandhi's writings distinguishing nonviolence from passive resistance as an admission that nonviolence is violent. See p. 227 for the passage and his interpretation.

34 Rosen, Michael, *Dignity: Its History and Meaning*, Cambridge: Harvard University Press, 2012.

35 Rosen, *Dignity*, pp. 61–2.

36 Robert Holmes, "Violence and Nonviolence," in *Violence: Award-Winning Essays in the Council for Philosophical Studies Competition*, ed. Jerome A. Shaffer (New York: David McKay Company, 1971), p. 111. Holmes argues that disrespect for persons is a matter of psychological violence, and so assimilates what we are calling here structural violence to psychological violence. This essay is reprinted in the collection referred to above in note 3 on pp. 149–68.

37 Deming, Barbara, "On Revolution and Equilibrium," *A.J. Muste Memorial Institute Essay Series*, no. 2, New York [originally published in Liberation Magazine, 1968], pp. 14–15.

38 Chenoweth and Stephan, *Why Civil Resistance Works*, p. 14.

39 For a description of this campaign, see Bondurant, *The Conquest of Violence*, pp. 46–52.

40 Schock, *Unarmed Insurrections*, p. xvii. Shock cites Robert Burrowes' *The Strategy of Nonviolent Defense: A Gandhian Approach* (New York: SUNY Press, 1996), pp. 98–101 as the source of his distinction.
41 This idea has its roots in Aristotelean literature on habituation. The locus classicus for this is Aristotle's own discussion in *The Nicomachean Ethics*, Book 1, Section 9, http://classics.mit.edu/Aristotle/nicomachaen.1.i.html

Chapter 3

1 Gandhi, M. K., *Non-Violent Resistance*, New York: Schocken Books, 1951, p. 3.
2 Chenoweth and Stephan, *Why Civil Resistance Works*, p. 7.
3 For a short but interesting account of these movements, see Mark Kurlansky's *Non-Violence: The History of a Dangerous Idea* (London: Jonathan Cape, 2006).
4 Gandhi, *Non-Violent Resistance*, p. 38.
5 Ibid., p. 42.
6 Bondurant, *The Conquest of Violence: The Gandhian Philosophy of Conflict*, Princeton: Princeton University Press, rev. ed. 1988 (or. pub. 1958), p. 9.
7 Bondurant, *The Conquest of Violence*, p. 11.
8 King, Martin Luther, *Why We Can't Wait*, New York: New American Library, 1963, p. 78.
9 Bondurant, *The Conquest of Violence*, p. 11.
10 Howes, Dustin Ellis, *Toward a Credible Pacifism: Violence and the Possibilities of Politics*, Albany: SUNY Press, 2009, p. 125.
11 Gregg, Richard, *The Power of Nonviolence*, Canton, Maine. Greenleaf Books (3rd edn, 1960), p. 44. One of the reviewers of this book when it was in manuscript noted that jiu-jitsu is probably not the best analogy, since in jiu-jitsu one does not allow oneself to receive the blows of the opponent. S/he suggest that Aikido might be a closer analogy. As a martial arts illiterate, I find this suggestion intriguing although, as the reviewer points out, jiu-jitsu has become the preferred analogy in the literature on nonviolence.
12 King, *Why We Can't Wait*, p. 30.
13 Ibid., pp. 79–80.

14 Sharp, Gene, *The Politics of Nonviolent Action*, Boston: Porter Sargent: 1973, p. 658.
15 Gandhi, *Non-Violent Resistance*, p. 181.
16 Bondurant, *The Conquest of Violence*, p. 197.
17 For a good short summary of the campaign, see Bondurant, *The Conquest of Violence*, pp. 46–52.
18 Gandhi, *Non-Violent Resistance*, pp. 185–6.
19 Bondurant, *The Conquest of Violence*, p. 50.
20 Ackerman and DuVall, *A Force More Powerful*, p. 390.
21 Bondurant, *The Conquest of Violence*, p. 11.
22 Sharp, *The Politics of Nonviolent Action*, p. 8.
23 Ibid., p. 12.
24 Ibid., p. 28.
25 King, *Why We Can't Wait*, pp. 63–4.
26 Sharp, *The Politics of Nonviolent Action*, p. 69.
27 Schock, *Unarmed Insurrections*, p. 8.
28 Sharp, *The Politics of Nonviolent Action*, p. 658.
29 For a detailed account of the Birmingham campaign, see especially Diane McWhorter's *Carry Me Home: Birmingham, Alabama, the Climactic Battle of the Civil Rights Revolution* (New York: Simon and Schuster, 2001). McWhorter grew up in Birmingham, and this history reflects her personal stake in what happened. For an account that places the Birmingham campaign in the context of the larger Civil Rights Movement, see Taylor Branch's magisterial *Parting the Waters: American in the King Years 1954–63* (New York: Simon and Schuster, 1988), esp. pp. 673–802.
30 King, *Why We Can't Wait*, pp. 80–1.
31 Schock, *Unarmed Insurrections*, p. 10.
32 Ibid., p. 49.
33 Ibid., p. 143.
34 Ibid., pp. 142–3.
35 Ibid., p. 151.
36 For a fuller account of Danish resistance to the Nazi occupation, see Ackerman and DuVall, *A Force More Powerful*, pp. 207–40.
37 Ibid., p. 223.
38 Ibid., p. 224.
39 For more on Critical Mass, see http://en.wikipedia.org/wiki/Critical_Mass_%28cycling%29

40 King, *Why We Can't Wait*, p. 5.
41 Gandhi, *Non-Violent Resistance*, p. 4.
42 Sharp, *The Politics of Nonviolent Action*, pp. 219–48.
43 For references on the effect of sanctions in Iraq, see the Wikipedia page on the issue: http://en.wikipedia .org/wiki/Sanctions_against_Iraq#Effects_on_the_Iraqi _people_during_sanctions. Joy Gordon's *Invisible War: The United States and the Iraq Sanctions* (Cambridge: Harvard University Press, 2010) provides an in-depth look at the history and effect of those sanctions.
44 Chenoweth and Stephan, *Why Civil Resistance Works*, pp. 213–15.
45 Ibid., p. 217.

Chapter 4

1 Schock, *Unarmed Insurrections*, p. 6.
2 Rosen, *Dignity*, p. 16.
3 Ibid., pp. 23–4.
4 Ibid., p. 54.
5 Ibid., pp. 61–2.
6 Kant, Immanuel, *Groundwork of the Metaphysic of Morals*, tr. H. J. Paton, New York: Harper and Row, 1964, p. 61.
7 Kant, *Groundwork*, p. 88.
8 Ibid., p. 96.
9 Ibid., p. 100.
10 Ibid., p. 101.
11 Ibid., p. 106.
12 Ibid., p. 102.
13 Ibid., p. 102.
14 Ibid., p. 102.
15 Ibid., p. 107.
16 I have written elsewhere on the moral status of nonhuman animals and what that requires of us. See my article, "Moral Individualism, Moral Relationalism, and Obligations to Non-human Animals," *Journal of Applied Philosophy*, currently on Early View, http://onlinelibrary .wiley.com/doi/10.1111/japp.12055/abstract
17 Bondurant, *The Conquest of Violence*, p. 29.
18 King, *Why We Can't Wait*, p. 29.
19 Bondurant, *The Conquest of Violence*, p. 230.

Chapter 5

1 *Inequality Reexamined.* Cambridge: Harvard University Press, 1992, p. ix.
2 Kant, Immanuel, *The Metaphysics of Morals,* tr. Mary Gregor. Cambridge: Cambridge University Press, 1991 [1797], p. 56.
3 Kant, Immanuel, *Groundwork of the Metaphysic of Morals,* tr. H. J. Paton. New York, Harper and Row, 1964 [1785], p. 96.
4 Kant, *Groundwork,* p. 100.
5 Sellars, Wilfrid, "Empiricism and the Philosophy of Mind," *Science, Perception, and Reality.* London: Routledge and Kegan Paul-Humanities Press, 1963, p. 170.
6 Rancière, Jacques, *The Ignorant Schoolmaster,* tr. Kristin Ross. Palo Alto: Stanford University Press, 1991 [1987], p. 46.
7 Kant, *Metaphysics of Morals,* p. 63.
8 Kant, *Groundwork,* p. 127. (We should probably note in passing that the relation of freedom to the moral law is articulated differently in the *Critique of Practical Reason,* where freedom is grounded in the "fact" of the moral law, but the key point at issue – that freedom is presupposed rather than demonstrated – remains.)
9 Rancière, Jaques, *Disagreement,* tr. Julie Rose. Minneapolis: University of Minnesota Press, 1999 [1995], pp. 29–30.
10 I am grateful to Mark Lance for suggesting the idea of performativity here, which replaces an earlier and less helpful formulation of mine.
11 Kant, *Metaphysics of Morals,* p. 52.
12 Rancière, *Disagreement,* p. 28.
13 Ibid., pp. 29–30.
14 Rancière, Jacques, *La Mésentente,* Paris: Editions Galilée, 1995, p. 57.
15 Kant, *Groundwork,* p. 67.
16 For a succinct but precise account of the Salt Satyagraha, see Bondurant, *The Conquest of Violence,* pp. 88–102. Gandhi's writings and pronouncement on it appear in Gandhi, *Non-Violent Resistance,* pp. 220–90.
17 Bondurant, *The Conquest of Violence,* p. 89.
18 Gandhi, *Non-Violent Resistance,* p. 262.

19 Cited in Bondurant, *The Conquest of Violence*, pp. 98–9.
20 Rancière, Jacques, *On the Shores of Politics*, tr. Liz Heron. London: Verso 1995 [1992], p. 48.
21 Sharp, *The Politics of Nonviolent Action*, p. 778.
22 *Disagreement*, p. 101.
23 Rancière, Jacques. *Hatred of Democracy*, tr. Steve Corcoran. London: Verso 2006 [2005], p. 41.
24 Howes, *Toward a Credible Pacifism*, p. 131.

Chapter 6

1 The following is a condensed version of my discussion of neoliberalism in *Friendship in an Age of Economics: Resisting the Forces of Neoliberalism*, Lanham, Maryland: Lexington Books, 2012, esp. chapter 1.
2 Harvey, David, *A Brief History of Neoliberalism*, Oxford: Oxford University Press, 2007, p. 2.
3 Harvey, *A Brief History of Neoliberalism*, p. 19.
4 There are several accounts of the Zapatista movement. My own, which links it to the work of Rancière, is in chapter 4 of May, *Contemporary Political Movements and the Thought of Jacques Rancière: Creating Equality*, Edinburgh: Edinburgh University Press, 2012.
5 For an early account, see http://www.nytimes.com/2003/07/08/world/workers-in-argentina-take-over-abandoned-factories.html For a slightly later and historically comprehensive account from a sympathetic observer, see http://sdonline.org/39/volume-19-no-3/argentina%E2%80%99s-worker-occupied-factories-and-enterprises/

Index